Understanding Research i Early Education

D0153649

It is easy to be blinkered by the pace of change and flood of documents on early education and care, and overlook the insights to be gained from past research.

Using the author's unique approach, this second edition of *Understanding Research in Early Education* examines and discusses both recent and historical research in understandable yet rigorous language, and a wide variety of large and small-scale research reports and projects are evaluated. Drawing on her own studies, as well as many others, Margaret Clark illustrates how to: avoid common pitfalls, ask the right questions to help inform students' own research projects and, critically, apply findings in the classroom or nursery to improve practice.

Without requiring any prior expertise in research and research methodologies, this book will prove invaluable and fascinating reading for undergraduate and postgraduate students taking courses in early years education, and practitioners undertaking continuing professional development.

Margaret Clark has an international reputation for research in early education and literacy. She is Emeritus Professor of Education, University of Birmingham and Visiting Professor at Newman College of Higher Education, Birmingham.

Understanding Research in Early Education

The relevance for the future of lessons from the past

2nd Edition

Margaret M. Clark

Visiting Professor, Newman College of Higher Education, Birmingham

Routledge
Taylor & Francis Group

LONDON AND NEW YORK

First edition published 1989
by Gordon & Breach

This edition published 2005 by Routledge
2 Park Square, Milton Park, Abingdon, Oxon OX14 4RN

Simultaneously published in the USA and Canada
by Routledge
270 Madison Ave, New York, NY 10016

Routledge is an imprint of the Taylor & Francis Group

© 1989, 2005 Margaret M. Clark

Typeset in Bembo by
Keyword Group Ltd

Printed and bound in Great Britain by
TJ International Ltd, Padstow, Cornwall

The right of Margaret M. Clark to be identified as the author of this work
has been asserted by her in accordance with the Copyright, Designs and
Patents Act 1988.

British Library Cataloguing in Publication Data
A catalogue record for this book is available
from the British Library

Library of Congress Cataloging in Publication Data
    Clark, Margaret MacDonald.
        Understanding research in early education: the relevance for the
    future of lessons from the past/Margaret M. Clark. – 2nd ed.
    p.cm.
    Includes bibliographical references and index.
    ISBN 0-415-36112-5 (hardback : alk. paper) – ISBN 0-415-36113-3
    (pbk. : alk. paper) I. Early childhood education – Great Britain –
    Evaluation. 2. Reading (Early childhood) – Great Britain – Evaluation.
    3. Children with disabilities – Education – Great Britain – Evaluation.
    I. Title.
    LB1139.3.G7C57 2005
    372.21'0941 – dc22   2005001118

ISBN 0-415-36112-5 (hb)
ISBN 0-415-36113-3 (pb)

Contents

Preface

The aim of this book is to bring research alive for a wide readership of those interested in early education, to remind readers of lessons from the past, enable them to evaluate current and future research and to plan research of their own. In this second edition of *Understanding Research in Early Education* I have adopted a similar style to the previous one: addressing readers personally, encouraging them to consider the present relevance of the researches being discussed and highlighting the issues.

Children Under Five: educational research and evidence (Clark 1988) was the report of a personal commission from the Secretary of State to undertake a critical evaluation of research in Britain of relevance to the education of children under five. *Understanding Research in Early Education* (Clark 1989) was addressed to students of early education, interpreting the term 'student' widely. The examples from research in that book were drawn mainly from my own research; studies in preschool units in Scotland, children who were already reading when they started school, studies of children with special needs in preschool units, and children from different ethnic backgrounds in schools in the West Midlands. Each research was set in its historical context, the reasons for the approach adopted were considered; more recent research was also identified.

Throughout my career I have undertaken research on issues I identified as of relevance to education, concurrently teaching undergraduates, training educational psychologists, and more recently master's degree courses for experienced practitioners. This has enabled me to introduce my students to ongoing research, enlist their help and encourage them to undertake related research for their projects. As you will see from the reference list, they were encouraged to publish articles based on their dissertations; these are marked with an asterisk. I appreciate that the reference list is very lengthy; even then it will have many omissions, for which I apologise. A number of important reports were due to appear as this manuscript went to the publisher; where possible I have alerted the reader to them.

Many of the researches analysed in my two books mentioned above appear on current reading lists, yet the original reports of most are now out of print, as are my two books. This second edition includes selected researches based on the previous edition, including the studies in preschool units and of young fluent readers, both undertaken in Scotland, and my study of children from different ethnic minorities undertaken in five primary schools in the West Midlands. The other chapters are modified sections from *Children Under Five: educational research and evidence*, including language in the homes of young children and in preschool units and on continuity from preschool to primary. These are set in their historical context and the current relevance of the findings considered.

The book has four sections and within each section there is an introductory chapter. Readers may find it helpful to read these chapters before embarking on the more detailed study of the researches; namely chapters 1, 2, 4, 7 and 10. Comments and questions to the reader are included in each chapter; these are highlighted in different print.

Margaret M. Clark
November 2004

Acknowledgements

I acknowledge with gratitude the support I have received from the Scottish Education Department, the Department of Education and Science and the local authorities in funding me and thus allowing me to conduct so many researches. I appreciate the fact that so few constraints were placed on me concerning how I conducted the researches and presented the reports. Without the funding, the commitment of my research teams and many students, administrators, staffs in the schools, and not least all the parents and children, it would not have been possible to have undertaken so many researches during my career. Thanks to help from my students, it was possible, while maintaining my teaching commitments, to undertake the wide range of research, complete it within the agreed timescale, and not least to report it in ways that are both meaningful to educationists and acceptable to fellow researchers. I acknowledge with particular gratitude the children, staffs and parents who have between them kept me in touch with the real world!

My thanks to my friends for their support, encouragement and their comments which have been invaluable; they have led to changes in both content and layout. Ann Lance and Professor Ann Lewis from Birmingham University encouraged me to write this new edition, have given helpful advice and drawn my attention to recent publications. Anne Farr at Newman College of Higher Education has helped personally and arranged for me to conduct discussion sessions on draft chapters with part-time BA Early Years Education students from Warwickshire, Walsall and the West Midlands in their final year at Newman College. Allison Tatton at Newman College has supported me not only by careful reading and helpful comments on drafts of the book, but by printing off chapters at crisis points when my printer failed! Lone Hattingh, a part-time PhD student whom I am supervising, in spite of her heavy teaching commitments, has also read the manuscript in draft form. Allison and Lone, recent classroom practitioners, have reassured me on the relevance of the issues explored in the book. Wendy Dewhirst, a friend and former colleague, has read and commented on the most recent draft to identify errors, repetitions or lack of clarity. Her positive reinforcement at this final stage has been particularly comforting; she also has fed me copies of the chapters when the printer failed!

Currently I feel it is a battle between me and the computer to complete the book on time!

Finally, my thanks to Routledge for agreeing to publish this book, in particular to Alison Foyle, the commissioning editor and to Alasdair Deas of Keyword for his helpful advice.

Margaret M. Clark

List of abbreviations

BERA	British Education Research Association
CREC	Centre for Research in Early Childhood
DES	Department of Education and Science
DfEE	Department for Education and Employment
DfES	Department for Education and Skills
EEC	Early Excellence Centre
EECERA	European Early Childhood Education Research Association
EEL	Effective Early Learning
EMSS	Ethnic Minority Support Service
EPPE	Effective Provision of Preschool Education
EPVT	English Picture Vocabulary Test
ESRC	Economic and Social Research Council
HMIE	Her Majesty's Inspectorate of Education (Scotland)
LEA	Local Education Authority
NAO	National Audit Office
NESS	National Evaluation of Sure Start
NFER	National Foundation for Educational Research
OfSTED	Office for Standards in Education (England)
PLAI	Preschool Language Assessment Instrument
PPVT	Peabody Picture Vocabulary Test
QCA	Qualifications and Curriculum Authority
REPEY	Researching Effective Pedagogy in the Early Years
SATs	Standard Assessment Tasks
SD	Standard Deviation
SED	Scottish Education Department
SEED	Scottish Executive Education Department
SIG	Special Interest Group
SSRC	Social Science Research Council

Introduction

In the rapidly changing educational scene it is easy to be blinkered by the pace of change and the flood of documents – and to fail to heed earlier warnings and insights into the development of young children. The early education and care of young children currently has a high profile with all political parties in the United Kingdom. The expansion in education and care for children under 5 years of age, and out-of-hours care for children in schools, has in part been driven by a desire to encourage more mothers of young children to enter the workforce, or to train to do so. Over recent years many of those concerned with early education have felt that balance and breadth in the curriculum in the early years in primary schools were being sacrificed in attempts to raise standards in literacy and numeracy and by the demand for primary schools, in England at least, to rank high in league tables. We can take comfort from not only the pledges of massive increases in funding, but also the curricular guidelines and other documents appearing that are aimed at improving the quality and breadth of education and care for children from an early age. The education and care of young children are among the devolved powers in the United Kingdom, therefore the documents come from Department for Education and Skills (DfES) for England, the Scottish Executive for Scotland and the Welsh Assembly for Wales. Priorities now include training of highly qualified staff, co-ordination of services and continuity of education as children transfer from home to school and from one stage of their education to the next.

In 1972 there was a commitment to increase the provision of preschool education for 3- and 4-year-olds, sadly changes in the economic climate meant that these promises were not fulfilled. However, the proposed expansion led to the funding of a programme of research to inform that expansion; many of these researches, undertaken in 1970s and 1980s, are still cited in current textbooks. Research can provide insights for policy and practice; there are lessons to be learnt from revisiting previous research to ensure we do not overgeneralize from limited evidence.

It seems timely to encourage current students of early education, and practitioners on advanced courses, to make a critical appraisal of previous research, to enable them to relate the findings to current issues and to gain a framework from which to plan their own investigations. This second edition of *Understanding Research in Early Education* is planned with these aims. It includes revised chapters from the previous edition (Clark 1989) and from *Children Under Five: educational research and evidence* (Clark 1988). The latter presented my evaluation of research of relevance to the education of children under 5 years old, based on a personal commission from the Secretary of State for Education. The topics I have chosen are of contemporary relevance, and although most of the researches were undertaken in England and Scotland, the issues they address are of concern to a much wider readership.

It is important that we 'demystify' educational research by showing that it can be presented in understandable, but rigorous language. My aim throughout is to show that research is understandable and interesting; that it is a continuous process where we ignore past insights at our peril; and that it is, or should be, relevant to policy and practice.

My aim is to bring research alive for the reader, while providing a source book and text relevant to courses on research. Before turning to the detailed analyses of the researches you might like to read the introductory chapters to each of the four sections of the book, namely chapters 2, 4, 7 and 10, to get a flavour of the contents. You will find that you are frequently addressed directly and encouraged to consider issues raised by the researches. These inserts are in different print; you may also like to glance at these before embarking on a detailed study. The approach is unusual in that you will find a dual focus: a critical analysis of classical studies by others and detailed reports of selected researches that I directed.

THE AIMS OF THE BOOK

The following are important features of this book:

- It is addressed particularly to students of early education (interpreting the term 'student' very widely).
- It is planned to be of interest to those concerned with children in the age range 3 to 7 or 8 years of age (at least).
- It presents researches on a variety of topics and with very different approaches, all of relevance to classroom practice.
- It analyses the decisions that were made in the course of planning and undertaking the researches.
- It shows how the approach and methodology of each study were influenced by its aims, and highlights the constraints that each approach placed on possible conclusions.
- Selected findings from each research are cited to give readers a flavour of the studies and to encourage students to wider reading on related topics.

- Each research is set in its historical context, both with regard to available choices of methodology and then current beliefs and interests.
- The researches are related to more recent developments, both in research and educational issues.

There are real dangers if, because of a crowded timetable, students experience only summaries of researches or brief statements of their findings. If that is their main diet, those involved may remain vulnerable to claims made from 'research evidence', provided these appear sufficiently impressive, for example because of large samples. Alternatively students may complete their courses unwilling to accept what are indeed new insights that are of value for practice.

I was engaged in funded research on a number of aspects of early education for over 20 years, in the 1970s and 1980s. In order to bring alive the realities of undertaking research on educational issues I have included for detailed discussion several of my own researches. My aim in this is to provide insights into the decision-making involved in planning and undertaking researches in education and the constraints that are faced by researchers. Throughout my career I was not only undertaking research on key issues, but was also lecturing to undergraduate and postgraduate students. I was thus able to introduce them to ongoing research, enlist their help in aspects of the research and encourage some of them to undertake dissertations related to the funded studies. I have referred to some of these dissertations, and also articles, by my students in the hope this will act as a stimulus to current students. Each of the researches is set in its historical context; thus indicating why I thought the investigation into each topic was of importance and why I adopted the approach I did.

You will find a very long reference list. It seemed important to retain the original references from the first edition; to these I have added more recent references, including where appropriate government policy documents with implications for early education.

WHAT DO WE MEAN BY RESEARCH

The term 'research' seems to be used in education in many different ways, and to refer to a wide range of approaches and types of enquiry. Among others it may refer to the following:

- so-called 'pure' experimental investigations in a laboratory or elsewhere
- surveys by questionnaire on a variety of topics
- interviews of adults or children, open-ended or semi-structured
- descriptive or qualitative case studies of schools or children
- observational and other studies in classrooms and homes
- recordings in homes or other settings
- practical work by students in training.

I have even seen the term used by some publishers in publicity leaflets in support of new materials (which I have then discovered were merely tried out in a few schools, rather than tested against existing or other new products). For some educational practitioners and policy-makers the word 'research' has an aura of respectability. For others it is seen as an academic exercise, undertaken by academics, with findings which are rarely even set in the real world of schools and classrooms, or which may not take account of the practicalities and limitations of educational decision-making. Much research is ignored by policy-makers; elements of other research may be used to justify condemnation of what practitioners may feel are educational advances. Likewise, the implementation of a policy, already decided on economic or political grounds, may be claimed to have the support of research. On occasion there may even be delay in the publication of the findings of commissioned research where these would sit uncomfortably alongside the pronouncements of the politicians!

Professionals should be able to distinguish fact from interpretation; not be misled by impressive language with which a research may be reported or elaborate statistical techniques with which the results may have been manipulated.

> You should be cautious in accepting the generalizations claimed by the researchers themselves; in particular be wary of press headlines or brief reports of the 'findings'. The more readily accessible and popular books containing reports of research may contain insufficient detail to allow critical evaluation or replication of the studies. Some of the mystique surrounding research must be laid at the door of researchers themselves. The journals and books in which researches are reported in sufficient detail for a critical evaluation of the findings may be difficult to access, and the language in which they are couched may be too technical for the general reader – it could even be jargon! The web may help you access a wider range of studies, but remember that anything and everything can appear on the internet; it is still necessary to acquire the skills to evaluate and be selective.

Contradictions in findings, or apparent contradictions between studies, may add to the confusion or distrust felt by practitioners and policy-makers. Where insufficient information is provided for replication of studies it may be even more difficult to assess the importance of evidence. Very few educational researches have been precisely replicated, sometimes because insufficient detail has been provided to make this possible. You should note that it is much more difficult to obtain funds to replicate a study than to undertake research on a different topic. There is a danger that the whole research exercise may be regarded as an exclusive club when viewed from the outside.

Being able to evaluate research is an important skill for professionals to acquire. Another important skill is the ability to access information; for some topics this may be a daunting task. There are numerous books on research methodology, but few that focus on the analysis of specific researches, and even fewer that deal with topics of specific relevance to early education. Two books that include critical evaluations of research involving children are *Doing Research with Children* (Greig and Taylor 1999) and *Making Decisions about Children: psychological questions and answers* (Schaffer 1990). Greig and Taylor stress the importance of evaluating the research of others; first, to be informed of the knowledge base from which you are working; second, to be able to use previous research intelligently when planning your own research. They stress that research training is much more than the undertaking of a small survey or experiment. Schaffer stresses the need to appreciate the limitations of research; to remember that not everything in print is 'good research' and that research is of necessity a slow affair. This is frustrating for policy-makers and practitioners, who want quick answers to immediate problems. He stresses that research should be regarded as a process of continuous updating (see Schaffer 1990: 7–21). Teachers, doctors and social workers are all urged to improve the quality of research, evaluate it more carefully and publicize it more widely, according to Aubrey, David *et al.* (2000), who claim that educational research in general, and early years educational research in particular, has never before been higher on the agendas of policy-makers. Teachers, they insist, should be prepared to read research reports, make informed judgements about them and then apply, if appropriate, the findings to their own work. There have recently been several reports with very critical evaluations of educational research, details of which are to be found in the above publication. They quote the following statement from Charles Clarke, made in 1999 when he was Schools Minister in England, that there is a 'discontinuity between research and what the government is doing and a widespread ignorance on what works and what doesn't in education as well as an effective data base that could provide answers to questions about schools, teaching and learning' (quoted in Aubrey, David *et al.* 2000: xi). It is comforting to find that Catherine Ashton, present Minister for Early Years and School Standards in England, in a recent article does quote research, namely, the findings from the Effective Provision of Preschool Education (EPPE) longitudinal research showing that preschool education can have an effect, especially where settings have well-qualified staff (Ashton 2004). In the same publication Jane Davidson, Minister for Education and Lifelong Learning, Wales, stresses the importance of early education and states that the 'new innovative and uniquely Welsh Proposals for A Foundation Phase for 3- to 7-year-olds are profound and far reaching and will give our youngest a flying start' (Davidson 2004: 4).

The aim in this book is to stimulate an interest in educational research and encourage professionals, even when their course is completed, to adopt a research perspective to their own practice and to that of others.

The stress is on acquiring a knowledge base from which to proceed, appreciating as Schaffer suggests that research is indeed a process of continuous updating.

> Most of the research discussed in the following chapters took place either in England or in Scotland. Note that there are major differences in education in Scotland. Education and care are among the responsibilities devolved to the Scottish Parliament and the Welsh Assembly. Be aware that the term 'reception class' is not used in Scotland, the equivalent class is Primary 1; Foundation Stage, Standard Assessment Tasks (SATs) and Key Stages, the Literacy Hour and Numeracy Hour do not apply to Scotland, and there have been no league tables for primary schools. The remit of the Office for Standards in Education (OfSTED) does not cover Scotland, where inspection is the responsibility of Her Majesty's Inspectorate of Education (HMIE); the Qualifications and Curriculum Authority (QCA) has no remit for Scotland, where Learning and Teaching Scotland is responsible for curricular innovation and issues documents in collaboration with the Scottish Executive. The National Curriculum is a curriculum for England; in Scotland there are curricular guidelines, currently covering ages 5–14, with proposals to revise these to cover ages 3–18. Both countries have issued a number of policy documents for preschool education, for ages 3–5 and birth–3. Bear these points in mind when reading educational research and considering its implications for policy. You will find these distinctions are seldom made in the media, even in some textbooks! (see Bryce and Humes 2003 for information on education in post-devolution Scotland).

OUTLINE

Chapter 1   The dual focus in the book and my aim of demystifying research for early-years practitioners are explained. The importance for practitioners of a research perspective and of studying researches in their historical context is argued. The danger of overgeneralization of findings if only the summaries of researches are studied is noted.

Section I   Language and the homes of young children

Chapter 2   Language was the major justification for the planned expansion of preschool education in 1970s, which was to some extent viewed as compensatory. One aim was for the professionals to make good deficiencies thought to arise from a lack of cognitively demanding language in the homes of many young children, though at that time there was little direct evidence from recordings in the homes. The terminology may have changed, yet some of these views on so-called 'disadvantaged children' and expectations of their likely progress may remain. Note an article in *The Guardian* under the heading 'Language cements a child's class destiny into place in its first three years' (Toynbee 2004: 8), and a study of three classrooms with different expectations and cultures (Gregory *et al.* 2004).

Chapter 3   The 1970s and 1980s saw the publication of pioneering studies comparing the language of middle-class and working-class young children in their homes and at preschool. Most of the publications giving details of the researches by Joan Tough, Gordon Wells, Barbara Tizard and Martin Hughes, John and Corinne Hutt and their colleagues are now out of print, though in 2002 a second edition of *Young Children Learning* (Tizard and Hughes 1984) was published. The researches evaluated in this chapter appear on many current reading lists (see for example Broadhead 1996; Aubrey, David *et al.* 2000; BERA 2003). For that reason, I decided to include my detailed evaluation of these researches from *Children Under Five: educational research and evidence* (Clark 1988).

Section II   Research in preschool units: what lessons can we learn?

Chapter 4   The context within which the researches funded for the proposed expansion of preschool education in 1970s had to be planned is considered, including the belief that a major aim for preschool education was to assist the language development of children from so-called 'disadvantaged homes'. A framework is set out to assist the reader to evaluate the researches reported in the two following chapters.

Chapter 5   A series of projects undertaken in the newly opened first nursery schools in a county in Scotland are discussed briefly. This research was a collaborative venture with some of the projects developing from our regular meetings with the head teachers of the units. One of the projects, on interest in books and stories, is considered in more detail. Lessons on the assessment of young children drawn from this research and their implications for current policy are also discussed.

Chapter 6   Two of the studies in preschool units funded within the Programme of Research and still cited are considered in this chapter; those in Oxfordshire directed by Jerome Bruner and those by Corinne and John Hutt and their colleagues. The findings and final report of the first large scale longitudinal British study into the effects of different types of preschool provision (EPPE) are due as I complete this manuscript (Sylva *et al.* 2004a; 2004b). Related research, Researching Effective Pedagogy in the Early Years (REPEY), and an extension of the research into the primary school are now underway. A brief discussion of this research is included, based on several of the technical papers and articles.

Section III Continuity, communication and learning in early education

Chapter 7 Continuity in the education of young children was one of the priority areas for research identified by the Department of Education and Science (DES) in 1975. Unfortunately the researches funded at that time tended to consider transition, rather than continuity, and to have a very short timescale. Many of the issues raised in the 1980s are still pertinent today. Although the ages of transition to different phases of education may vary across the years, and also in different countries, this is a highly topical issue where there are lessons to be learnt from previous research. Many of the papers presented at the European Early Childhood Research Association (EECERA) conference in Malta in 2004 dealt with some aspect of transition, either within preschool settings or from one phase of education in the primary school to another. In England, for example, this might involve change from the Foundation Stage to Year 1, and the National Curriculum. In the expectations placed on the children and the parents at the move from one phase of education to the next, conflict rather than continuity was revealed in many of the studies. This chapter provides a framework within which to consider how true this remains today. (See *Transitions*, edited by A.-W. Dunlop and H. Fabian (2003) for a series of papers from different countries.)

Chapter 8 This and the following chapter discuss a research that I directed into various aspects of the early education of children from different ethnic minorities in five schools in the West Midlands. Evidence of the children's apparent ability to communicate in different settings is based on tests and recordings of selected children at the preschool stage, within the reception classroom with their teachers, in the playground and in groups with their peers.

Chapter 9 Learning in school takes place in a social context that includes a large number of children of about the same age, though the age range may vary from one school to another; their competing needs must be met by the teacher. The focus in this chapter is on the similarities and differences in reception classrooms as contexts for learning. This was explored by observations in the classrooms and interviews with the teachers and some of the parents.

Section IV What can we learn from children who succeed?

Chapter 10 The context for two contrasting researches on learning to read which I directed is set in this chapter. Textbooks from 1970s represented reading as a mainly visual skill, acquired in the first few years in primary school; being explicitly taught, then practised, extended and later developed into silent reading for comprehension. The focus was on different methods of teaching initial reading, on contrasts between children who succeed and those who fail, and reading readiness tests. Learning to read was *not* seen to concern practitioners in preschool units, those working in the upper stages of junior schools or in secondary schools. Changing views on reading and learning to read are considered; many of the studies discussed are still on reference lists in current textbooks (for example Hall *et al.* 2003 and Whitehead 2004).

Chapter 11   Two contrasting researches are discussed, the first a large-scale community study of children with continuing reading difficulties; the second an in-depth study of young children who started school at 5 years of age already reading fluently and with understanding. These are used to illustrate the need for very different approaches to research depending on the aims. *Young Fluent Readers* (Clark 1976), the report of my research, though it is now out of print, is still frequently cited and was the stimulus for a recent study in England after the introduction of the National Curriculum. That research involved a follow-up to the end of Key Stage 2 of children already reading fluently on entry to school compared with a control group (Stainthorp and Hughes 1999; 2004).

Chapter 12   The extent to which developments over the past 25 years have taken account of research findings and the recommendations of the various committees is considered. Research priorities are identified, including the importance of research into continuity in the early education of young children rather than merely transition from home to school, or from one stage of education to another, which has been the focus in most researches so far. The importance of improved management skills in those who will lead the pioneering new developments, and committed highly trained professionals to implement any new curricular proposals, is noted. Finally, the need for a real partnership between the adults responsible for the care and education of young children is emphasized, with a central role for the parents and an appreciation of their contribution to their children's development.

Section 1

Language and the homes of young children

Chapter 2

The language of young children
Perceptions in the 1970s and their continuing relevance

THE SCENE IN THE 1970s

A study of the literature from the 1970s reveals that preschool education in particular was regarded as the solution to educational disadvantage. In this chapter I have deliberately introduced in quotes many of the terms in frequent use at that time, both in Britain and in the United States.

Language was a major justification for the planned expansion in pre-school education in the 1970s in Britain. To some extent such education was viewed as 'compensatory' to give a 'head start' to children who were 'socially disadvantaged' because of perceived 'deficient' language thought to be responsible for later failure in school. Some researchers linked this to a lack of 'cognitively' demanding language in their homes, with the use of 'restricted' rather than 'elaborated' codes. Thus the aim for professionals was to make good the 'deficiencies of the home' at an early stage, preferably before entrance to primary school. Little or no attention was directed to possible links between school and its approaches and the differential attainments of children from so-called 'middle' and 'working' classes, or indeed the increasing gulf in their attainments as they moved through compulsory schooling.

> Consider what explanations are given now for the differential attainments of children from different social classes and the fact that the gap increases as the pupils proceed through their education? Make a list of any home and school features you think might be responsible.

I have been selective in the references in this chapter, citing mainly official reports and collected writings. Some appreciation of the views of the time can be gained from the Plowden Report, *Children and their Primary Schools*, volume 2 of which reports research and surveys (DES 1967) and the Bullock Report, *A Language for Life* (DES 1975a: ch. 5). Nisbet and Watt in *Educational Disadvantage: ten years on* (1984) indicate the inevitably of disenchantment with education as the solution in view of the impossibility of the task it was set, much of the focus being on preschool education. In a further report 10 years later on these authors stress that educational disadvantage is a matter of continuing concern, however with new priorities and partnerships (Nisbet and Watt 1994).

There were disputes as to how the 'disadvantaged child' should be taught, whether by programmes, and if so how structured they should be. The deficiencies shown to exist in standardized test situations, and also in less formal 'contrived' situations with an adult, were thought by some to result from the children's lack of knowledge of language 'structures'. Others thought that these 'deficiencies' were in 'language in use' by children who had already acquired the structures, although they seldom, or perhaps never, used them in settings with a strange adult. If it were the former deficiency then in order to make up for lost time didactic 'structured language programmes' might be essential. If the latter, more experience of dialogue with professional adults, who set a more cognitively demanding framework, could be required. Bernstein was the name most often cited in connection with restricted language use of 'working-class' children. Among those influenced by his writings was Joan Tough, whose research will be discussed in the next chapter.

In seeking to give 'positive discrimination' to disadvantaged children in Britain certain districts or areas were identified for 'priority' in funding, in many instances for preschool services, thus the concept of 'Educational Priority Areas' was used for funding of 'action research', and also for urban aid. The view that the best way to give positive discrimination is to identify areas of deprivation and then place extra preschool resources in these areas was shown to be simplistic and to lead to provision for the less disadvantaged who happen to live in these areas; seldom did it reach those in greatest need.

Make a list of the terms I have included in this chapter and consider how many are still in use today. Can you think of any further expressions now used to classify those for whom educational failure is frequently predicted?

In the 1970s voices were already being raised in opposition to the views cited above, with their implications of incompetence for the families and the children; several writers made reference to 'the myth of the deprived child'. Three important papers in a collection entitled *Language and Poverty* reflect some of these points (see Cazden 1970, Labov 1970 and Bernstein 1970, all in Williams 1970). Cazden stresses the need to consider the topic, the task and the listener (particularly their age in relation to that of the speaker) in any assessment of a child's language competence. Labov criticizes the assumptions of deficiency in non-standard (black) English, arguing persuasively that such language can be used in dynamic and cognitively demanding ways. Bernstein challenges assumptions that preschool education on its own can make good deficiencies resulting from social disadvantage. Significantly he also challenges the use of the term 'compensatory' education for children whom he claims have not yet been offered an adequate educational environment. Unfortunately, Bernstein became known to many teachers and their trainers only in connection with the expressions 'elaborated' and 'restricted' code as a dichotomy to distinguish the language of middle-class and working-class children. Yet it should be noted that much of the evidence cited was in experimental, contrived situations, not based on studies in the children's homes.

Some of Bernstein's co-workers did develop practical ways of working with children in classrooms. Robinson, one of those who worked with Bernstein, has suggested persuasively that one of the possible influences on the progress, or lack of progress, of children from so-called 'disadvantaged homes' may be the teachers' judgements and expectations of them. This at an early stage is likely to be influenced by the children's oral language use, in particular their responses in the formal classroom situation. Such judgements may be formed early and may indeed influence the children's concepts of themselves. This could be an alternative explanation, or at least an additional factor, of relevance to the increasing gulf in attainment as children move through primary school (Robinson 1980). The evidence on language in the homes of young children, based on observations and recordings, as it became available made this latter argument more persuasive.

> What factors do you think influence the early judgements that teachers make of the language competence of young children? In what ways might such views affect their expectations of the children and the children's own self-esteem?

At the time of the initial expansion of preschool provision in the 1970s there was little evidence based on studies of language in the homes of preschool children, nor were there many longitudinal studies of young children. The language the parents used at home had often been extrapolated from the way they conducted themselves in interviews with teachers or other 'strange' adults. Assessment of the language of young children was frequently based on standardized language tests or intelligence tests, not observation of their interactions with their peers or parents. Already by the 1960s there were challenges to the appropriateness of such as measures of 'innate' ability, particularly of young children. Attention was beginning to be drawn to the susceptibility of such tests to environmental influences, their cultural specificity and fluctuations in scores when young children were tested. It was even suggested that changes in scores over time might represent real changes and not merely unreliability of the instruments (see *Intelligence and Experience*, Hunt 1961). With reference to fluctuations in the scores of young children, see *Studies in Preschool Education* (Clark and Cheyne 1979).

Two further publications dealing with these issues are *Language and Learning in Early Childhood* (Davies, A. 1977), which contains papers from two Social Science Research Council (SSRC) seminars and the discussion surrounding them. Those who presented papers included Cazden from the United States, to whom reference has already been made (Cazden 1977). *Helping Communication in Early Education* (Clark 1985a) has papers from a seminar in which researchers such as Bogle from Jamaica and Katz and Blank from the United States discuss the implications of their work for our understanding of young children's language. Practical studies undertaken by my students and research that I directed are also reported in the latter publication.

RECENT DEVELOPMENTS

There has been a resurgence of interest in the work of Bernstein. His theories, although influential in the 1970s and 1980s, had been highly controversial. The four volumes of his *Class, Codes and Control* (published between 1971 and 1990) have recently been reprinted (Bernstein 2003) and a new book has appeared entitled *Reading Bernstein, Researching Bernstein* (Davies *et al.* 2004). Gregory and her colleagues, in their longitudinal study of young children from very different backgrounds attending three schools with contrasting philosophies represented in their approaches to learning in the early years, identify Bernstein as one of those whose views influenced their theoretical stance (Gregory *et al.* 2004).

A longitudinal research in the United States in which language interactions were recorded over a period of 2 years in the homes of very young children, up to the age of three, has recently gained considerable publicity on both sides of the Atlantic (Hart and Risley 1995). The sample for this study was 42 families, 13 classified as professional, 23 working-class and 6 on welfare; 29 of these children were followed through school to the age of nine or ten. A new insertion, 'A Preface for 2002', in the 2002 reprint has attracted the attention of journalists in Britain. The authors make the claim that: 'If children could be given better parenting, intervention might be unnecessary' (Hart and Risley op. cit.: 130).

> What do you think that might imply? I have deliberately used it out of context to alert you to the danger of accepting isolated comments. Embedded in their chapter 'Equalizing early experience', the authors give it a very different interpretation from that you might have anticipated.

According to these authors, 'the problem of skill differences among children at the time of school entry is bigger, more intractable, and more important than we had thought' (Hart and Risley op. cit.: 193). Furthermore they argue that their findings are predictive of the children's subsequent attainment in school. An article by Polly Toynbee that appeared in *The Guardian* has as its heading 'We can break the vice of the great unmentionable' and a sub-heading

'Language cements a child's class destiny into place in the first 3 years'. She goes on to claim from the research that intervention works.

> Give very young children intensive interaction with teachers and they make up for what they lack at home; parents can easily be taught to read and talk to their young children constructively. IQ, they say, is only a measure of the child's early experience and that can be changed.

> (Toynbee 2004: 8)

As this shows, categorization by class is not merely a view from the 1970s!

In the following chapter evidence from four British researches on the language of preschool children will be summarized and evaluated. The four studies, those of Tough, Wells, Tizard and Hughes and John and Corinne Hutt and colleagues, are still cited in relation to the language in the homes of young children and how this might influence their needs within early education (BERA 2003). It is important to remind early educators what these researches did and did not show and the fact that in some secondary sources the findings are overstated or generalized beyond what is legitimate from the samples on which they are based.

I hope after reading my analyses in the following chapters you will appreciate how complex this problem is, it is not one that will be solved by simplistic interventions. Rather than providing you with a detailed evaluation of the research by Hart and Risley, after discussing the four researches noted above I will alert you to the issues you need to consider in evaluating more recent researches such as these.

Chapter 3

Research evidence on language and the homes of young children

Looking back and looking forward

INTRODUCTION

This chapter is a modified version of Chapter 5 of *Children Under Five: educational research and evidence* (Clark 1988), now out of print. Four British researches are summarized and evaluated to help readers to assess how widely their results can be generalized. The four studies, by Tough, Wells, Tizard and Hughes and Corinne and John Hutt and their colleagues, although they took place in the 1970s, continue to influence our views on the language of young children and of their homes. The research by Tizard and Hughes, as reported in *Young Children Learning* (Tizard and Hughes 1984), in particular is cited in many textbooks currently used in courses for early years educators; the second edition, which appeared as recently as 2002, still reports the same study. Assumptions about the language of young children prevalent when these studies were undertaken were discussed in Chapter 2.

> This evaluation should help you develop a critical framework from which to assess researches and plan your own. Check how many of these researches are cited in textbooks, and after reading this chapter consider whether the claims made for them are justified. It would be useful to make notes on each study in turn as this will help with subsequent comparisons.

THE DEVELOPMENT OF MEANING: TOUGH

Joan Tough's study of the language of preschool children was completed by the early 1970s. She was then funded by Schools Council until 1983 to develop curriculum materials for language work with young children, also by DES, within the programme of research from 1976 for a study entitled 'Fostering the Development and Use of Language by Young Children'. She prepared videos and training materials for teachers and others working with young children; these were widely used. Her work is referred to in DES 1975a and 1975b. Tough's was one of the very few curriculum or compensatory projects to be derived from a prior study of development. In *A Language for Life* (DES 1975a) she cites her categorization of purposes for which language is used, and the differences she found between her 'advantaged' (middle class) and 'disadvantaged' (working class) samples. To quote: 'But there is a range of uses which children from "educating" homes seem to have developed more extensively than children without these home advantages' (DES 1975a: 53). It is claimed that in Tough's work there is confirmation of what was found in many other British and American researches. (See the previous chapter for a discussion of these issues.) It is further stated that: 'A child is at a disadvantage in lacking the means to explain, describe, inquire, hypothesize, analyse, compare, and deduce if language is seldom or never used for these purposes in his home . . . and that such abilities are important for learning in the school situation' (DES 1975a: 54).

There are many publications by Tough or which cite the longitudinal study she undertook; however, only one publication gives details of the research study. Even that publication, *The Development of Meaning* (Tough 1977), is not a research report in any strict sense as it does not contain the full information for an evaluation of the findings.

The sample

The study was a longitudinal investigation of a group of 64 children, samples of whose language in 'contrived' situations arranged by the researcher were tape recorded and analysed at the ages of 3, 5+ and 7+ years. There were two groups, referred to as the 'advantaged' and 'disadvantaged' groups, within each of which was a group who attended nursery school or class and a group not attending (each of the four groups had equal numbers of boys and girls). Data was collected from additional children to provide replacements for children in the original groups who might become inaccessible later.

The advantaged group had one or both parents from 'professions which are generally reached through a course in higher education' (teachers, doctors, lawyers and others of similar status). The disadvantaged group had parents who 'completed their education at the minimum age, and worked in unskilled, or semiskilled occupations' (Tough 1977: 2).

Excluded from the sample were children:

- whose IQ was below 105
- from a family of more than six children
- who showed evidence of known or suspected rejection or emotional stress
- whose mother did not speak English as her first language

- who were West Indian, because of problems with use of non-standard English
- were shy, withdrawn or hostile to the observer
- in the nursery if they were not happily settled in school
- did not speak clearly enough for transcriptions to be made of what they said.

> Note that it was difficult to find children for the advantaged group who were not in some form of preschool, and also that the composition of the group had excluded the most disadvantaged section of the population. Consider how that might limit the generalizability of the findings.

Teachers in nursery schools and classes were asked to select children who fitted the criteria. The non-nursery children were selected initially by the head teachers of infant schools, who were asked to identify families who might have children who would fit the criteria. These schools were in areas where there were no nursery schools or classes available, schools which 'served the large housing estates on the edge of the city, or the "down town" areas of the city' (Tough 1977: 4).

Thus this study is of children in an urban area, the city is not named and details are not given of the pattern and proportion of children who attended preschool education at that time (about 1970). Tough makes reference on page 130 to the children living in 'Yorkshire towns and cities'. The precise arrangement for the selection of the advantaged is not indicated. Clearly a final process of exclusion of children referred was still open to the investigator. All the above points about the sample are important yet are not normally noted in secondary sources.

> Make a note of key aspects of the sample in each of the researches which are important should you wish to compare the findings with other studies. Include anything for which details are *not* provided.

Samples of language

At 3 years of age each child was recorded in conversation with a 'chosen companion' with a collection of play materials. An observer was present during the approximately 1 hour of recording. The observer's role is referred to, but there is only passing reference to its possible importance, which could have been differential. There is reference to the extent to which the group addressed the adult. It is clear from extracts of dialogue that the adult, by her very presence, would have influenced the dialogue. At a later stage in the study the adult did leave children to talk in her absence, but not at 3 years of age.

Little attention is given in the report to possible effects of the 'chosen companion'; this might have been differential. Dialogue is a two-way process, not only one child (the target child) would initiate. Likewise language surrounding imaginative play depends on reciprocity between the two participants. It is possible that the chosen companions of the advantaged children were more likely themselves to be advantaged and those of the disadvantaged similar to the target child. Two extracts are given as a context for discussion and categorization, a brief extract from Billy and Michele and a longer extract from Tom, Sally and the observer (Tough 1977: 72–7), which make such a suggestion at least plausible.

> Note that the adult's presence appeared to affect the groups differentially. Consider what might have been the effect if all the advantaged children had played with a less-advantaged playmate and all the disadvantaged had the benefit of a more-advantaged companion. Note the influence of the context, the task set, whether there were probes and with whom the children were interacting on the children's apparent language competence. Because the tasks were different at the successive ages, developmental trends in language in use cannot be deduced from this research although it was longitudinal. Note that longitudinal research involves following the same sample of children over a period of years. In cross-sectional research different age groups may be studied, but not the same children.

The findings

This study was a pioneering attempt to record and analyse the language of a relatively large sample of young children in as near natural settings as seemed possible at that time, rather than by tests. However, it is important to bear in mind the highly selective nature of both samples of children:

- Only those who already spoke clearly were included; thus there could be many children entering preschool education at 3 years of age, or even infant school at 4 or 5 years of age, whose language structure and use is even more limited than the most-limited cited in that report, at least in such contexts.
- There is no way of knowing from the description of this sample just how selective it is from the point of view of articulation. Thus teachers may well be faced with many children who on entry to school have articulation so poor that their communicative attempts are difficult for the adults and their peers to follow.
- One may assume that the 'chosen companions' also spoke clearly, which would also influence the quality of language elicited from the 3-year-olds.
- Differences in competence between the chosen companions could also have affected the extent to which dialogue was sustained and imaginative play developed in pairs of children.

There are still insights from this research for present-day early educators. One important finding, which is mentioned less frequently and yet is of crucial importance, is *the effect of the context on the children's apparent competence*. The data from the children at 3 years of age does not allow such information to be extracted, as only one setting was used, and that setting was not used at 5+ and 7+. Within age groups differences were found at this later stage. Particularly important was that the gap, even between the means of the advantaged and disadvantaged groups, was much narrower in some settings than in others.

> Teachers who utilize only limited contexts from which to judge young children's language competence may assume a wider gulf between the less-advantaged, for whom some such situations may be unusual, unknown or alien, and the more-advantaged, for whom they may be common everyday experiences within which they comfortably express their views at length to an adult or other child.

At 5 years and 7 years of age there were striking differences in the groups in the complexity with which they expressed interpretations of a picture, the more-advantaged it is claimed 'injected meaning into the situation' (Tough 1977: 101). The disadvantaged children tended to give short responses which treated the picture as a series of objects, and thus it is argued that 'the children were orientated to examine the situations differently' and so used 'different strategies of language' (Tough 1977: 103). Such evidence is important because it shows that even in such a highly selected group of 'disadvantaged' children response to such commonly used materials as pictures, unless supported and encouraged, may lead only to labelling of unrelated objects. This may be reinforced by use of pictures of discrete objects where a labelling response may be all that is required by the teacher!

In a section entitled 'Some contradictions' in a chapter called 'Language and disadvantage at school' Tough makes crucial points for understanding the language knowledge and use of young children (based on the evidence from the children at 7+ years of age).

- For all the activities except free conversations the disadvantaged children's utterances tend to be considerably shorter than those of the advantaged children.
- The advantaged children talked more than the disadvantaged in these settings and the difference 'was greater when imaginative projection was asked for' (Tough 1977: 157–8).
- When retelling a story the disadvantaged children had a mean length of utterance which was almost twice as high as in other situations. They showed they were able to remember sequences and reproduce the story line with much of the detail (note: the story was repeated to a companion in a meaningful context).

Note the difference in types of response to pictures. When retelling a story in a meaningful context the disadvantaged children's mean length of utterance was almost twice as high as in other situations. You might record the response of young children to pictures and when retelling a story and see whether you find differences comparable to those reported by Tough. Are you able to improve the level of the children's functioning by applying any of the insights from this research?

Tough expresses caution at the ways in which linguistic data should be interpreted because, although the disadvantaged children showed lower mean scores, for all measures:

- the range of scores was not necessarily less, and
- all the children produced long, complex utterances at times.

When retested at 7 years of age the IQs of the disadvantaged group were lower than when initially tested at 3 years of age. They were inclined for some types of items to respond with 'I don't know', or otherwise avoid answering the question. Thus the tests may be an underestimate of their knowledge and understanding. It may not be 'a lack of resources of language that governs what they do. The child's disadvantage in school seems to stem more from a lack of motivation to think in those ways...' (Tough 1977: 165–6).

One major difference between the children in these groups in these situations appears to be, according to Tough, 'in their disposition to use language for particular purposes'. Frequently when pressed further the disadvantaged children 'moved towards the answer given spontaneously by the children in the advantaged groups' (Tough 1977: 170). To quote:

> All that can be inferred from this is that in this context, and others that were used, the children in the disadvantaged groups did not refer to past experience as explicitly and readily as did the advantaged groups.
>
> (Tough 1977: 111)

Clearly in many situations in school, children are likely to be judged by the more limited responses and this may in turn lead to lowered expectations – perhaps in the way suggested in the articles referred to in the previous chapter by Cazden (1970) and Robinson (1980).

As was noted earlier the initial sampling for this study was such as to ensure half of the children in each group attended nursery school or class. The children in the nursery groups were selected from 11 different nursery schools and classes, supervised by experienced teachers. No detail is given as to whether the advantaged and disadvantaged groups were in the same, or similar preschool units (as was the case in the study by Tizard and Hughes to be discussed later). The first recordings, at 3 years of age, were made shortly after the children had started in preschool education. At that stage there were already some statistically significant differences between the nursery and non-nursery disadvantaged groups. Tough suggests this may be explained by the fact that the children in the nursery schools and classes were already gaining experience of talking with a friend in the presence of an adult. Even were that the only explanation, it could have important implications.

> A 'disadvantaged' child who had experience of preschool education might on entry to infant school reveal to the teacher, even without probing, greater apparent competence in language situations in the classroom which might in turn result in increased expectations of the child. Consider the importance of these comments for testing and questioning of young children. This will be discussed further in chapters 5 and 8.

It is difficult to evaluate the significance of this study with regard to nursery attendance and its effects on language as only a few pages are devoted to this discussion (Tough 1977: 170–2). Little detail is provided on the comparability of the groups in relation to the nursery education they received, on date of entry to infant school or similarity of language experiences in school between the ages of 5 and 7 years.

Implications for early education

> It is stressed that the situation, and also whether there were probes, influenced the children's language differentially and that there was considerable overlap between the groups. The discussion tends, however, to be in terms of means, as was so common at that time, and the extracts which are cited appear to be selected to show contrasts between groups. It would have been valuable had some examples been cited of less successful advantaged children and of individual children in the disadvantaged group who were successful.

Parental interviews could have been used to put 'flesh' on to such studies. One unfortunate effect of Tough's approach in presentation, and of the classification of uses of language which she developed, is that in most secondary sources it is only to this classification that reference is made. Reference is often to absolute differences between advantaged and disadvantaged children in their uses of language and the need to teach the latter what the former have grasped already. There *are* successful children from 'disadvantaged' homes and less-successful children from advantaged homes. Even with such highly selected groups as in this study one feels there may have been some hidden within the mean scores. This was certainly true in the larger and more representative sample from Bristol in the studies by Wells, discussed later in this chapter. A study of young children who were already able to read with understanding on entry to school, at 5 years of age, also included some who were from so-called 'disadvantaged homes' (see Clark 1976 and Chapter 11).

Joan Tough was influenced by the work of Bernstein and by the views of Piaget, to whom she refers frequently. The experimental work of Donaldson was only beginning to appear when Tough's researches were published. Donaldson was able to show that, even in experiments such as those on which Piagetian evidence was based, the precise context will influence the child's apparent competence (see *Children's Minds*, Donaldson 1978). As was noted earlier, for many years the work of Bernstein was highly controversial; however, recently there has been a renewed interest, with the reprinting of the four volumes of his work and the publication of an edited book (see Bernstein 2003 and Davies *et al.* 2004).

A CRITIQUE BY WELLS OF TOUGH'S RESEARCH FINDINGS

Gordon Wells, whose research I will consider next, made a critique of Joan Tough's research in direct response to *The Development of Meaning* (Tough 1977). He raises the issue as to whether such marked differences as Tough found between her groups could have been 'an artefact of the way in which the groups were selected' (Wells 1977: 3); thus whether the conclusions would be supported were the full spectrum of family backgrounds from which the school population was drawn to be studied. Wells selected from his own sample a group to give equal representation to four classes of family background across the full spectrum, using the same criteria of occupation and education of both parents. Four boys and four girls in each group were studied (with no cut-off for IQ or exclusion of children). The recordings were of *spontaneous speech* in the home, which was then analysed as described by Tough. According to Wells, the Bristol data revealed large *within-group differences*, particularly for the more complex categories, and much smaller differences between classes, 'with very few cases of a clear trend over all four classes of family background (Wells 1977: 4–5). Wells raises issues similar to those I have raised, including:

- the danger of making generalizations about habitual use of language from speech samples in one limited situation
- the danger of claiming from later evidence in different but also limited situations that the differences between the groups in habitual use of language had increased
- that all the situations were 'non-spontaneous' and one cannot assume that each child's perception of the task was the same

- that because a child did not use, or seldom used, certain forms of language in these situations it cannot be inferred that they would not do so in a different setting with different communication partners.

The above points concerning young children's language were confirmed in studies by the present author (see chapters 5 and 8). Language samples collected in a variety of contexts using radio microphones revealed wide differences in the child's apparent competence; indeed we found some of the most complex language in discussion around relevant tasks in a 'contrived' situation but with peers, with no adult involved; the arrival of the adult affected the dialogue as the children began to defer to her.

One further point which Wells makes is the danger of assuming that educational success can be predicted for individual children by means of the type of categorization in the Tough study. He discusses what variables were found to be predictive in his sample. Finally, Wells stresses, based on his language samples from young children's spontaneous conversations at home, that the type of dialogue which Tough refers to as 'enabling' occurs rarely, even in the more-advantaged homes (see also the studies by Davie, Hutt and others, described later in this chapter). What he feels to be important for sustaining dialogue is 'the presence or absence of genuine reciprocity and collaboration' (Wells 1977: 10). Should this prove to be the case, and there is now further evidence to support this view, then it will also have important implications for stimulation of language in young children.

> Consider the possibility that dialogue with adults in a 'contrived' situation, that is one arranged for the purpose of talk, may merely serve to reinforce teachers' ideas about children's limitations, which a wider knowledge of these children might have dispelled.

STUDIES OF LANGUAGE AT HOME AND AT SCHOOL: WELLS

These studies by Wells, and related studies by co-workers, were extensively funded between 1972 and 1984 by, among others, SSRC (and later ESRC) and the Nuffield Foundation, and latterly by DES also. Numerous articles on the studies were produced by Wells and by his co-workers during the period of the grants and later a series of books was also produced. The sources from which most of the following information has been taken are the later books (Wells 1985 and 1986), and also the unpublished 1984 report to DES, *Linguistic Influences on Educational Attainment*. Here I have limited reference to two of Wells' publications, those of 1985 and 1986 (for further information see Clark 1988).

The Bristol study began as an investigation of language development with two main aims:

- to describe the sequence of language development in a sample of children learning to speak English as their first language
- to investigate the environmental factors that might have an influence on that development.

It was also hoped to describe these children's conversational experience and to investigate the relationship between preschool experience and success in school.

The sample

A pilot study was undertaken in 1971–2 and the main study commenced in 1973. Full details of the sample are set out in Wells 1985: ch. 1. The sample was drawn from City of Bristol birth records of children born in 1969–70 and 1971–2. Those excluded initially were children:

- of multiple births
- with known handicaps
- whose parents were not native speakers of English
- who were in institutions or full-time day care
- likely to move soon
- who had siblings already in the study.

The sample consisted of 128 children from a larger randomly drawn sample in Bristol of children representative in sex, month of birth and family background (based on occupation and education of both parents). Half of the sample was aged 15 months and half 39 months at the start of the research. A sample of 32 children from the younger group was followed into school and over their first 2 years in primary school, and a further assessment was made when the children were aged 10 years 3 months. A first visit to seek agreement was made by a health visitor; after excluding the children in the above groups and those whose parents refused to be interviewed by the researchers, 63.4 per cent of the initial pool was left (see Wells 1985: 26–7). The commitment required was then explained to these families, and of those interviewed 87.4 per cent agreed to take part (more of those who refused were in lower social classes). Age of the children was spread through the year, with selection from 8 months of birth. Random selection was then used to enable appropriate patterns with regard to the grouping by occupation and education of parents, month of birth and sex. Additional children were included as replacements. Details are given of any withdrawals after an initial observation; these were selective in ways that gave concern to the research team (e.g. more boys than girls). However, the final sample of 125 (of the 128) children for whom few observations were missing did cover:

- a younger and older age group
- a spread across the year in date of birth
- a range of family backgrounds
- roughly equal numbers of boys and girls, both in the total and within each category.

Other features of the children and their backgrounds were allowed to vary randomly but details are given on some aspects in Wells' chapter 'The children and their families', in which the parental interviews are also reported (Wells 1985: ch. 7).

Outline of the research

The study of language pre-school involved sampling (by means of a radio microphone) of *naturally occurring conversation*, which was sampled in 90-second spells for a complete day from 9 a.m. until 6 p.m. once every three months over a period of two-and-a-quarter years. There was no observer present during these recordings and contexts were identified by replaying the tapes to the parents at the end of each day.

> Consider any limitations this approach would put on the language and its interpretation.

Wells found that although the 'route' of the children's language development was similar there were wide differences in the rate of development, which appeared to be related to the quality of the 'child's conversational experience'.

> The quality and quantity of the conversational experience was the best predictor of the child's oral language at entry to primary school. Furthermore, attainment at 7 years of age could be strongly predicted by differences between children on entry. The more recent American study by Hart and Risley, which will be discussed at the end of this chapter, drew similar conclusions. These authors refer to the work of Wells.

Wells attempted to identify aspects of conversation that appeared to be related to later attainment in school at 7 years of age, and in particular 'literacy related' activities. Those he found to be the most powerful in their effects were the contexts related to story; the implications for education of this are discussed in a number of publications, for example in *The Meaning Makers* (Wells 1986). Through data from the longitudinal study, Wells states that one of the most important features found in the homes of children whose success could have been predicted early was 'the sharing of stories'. This he suggests, in relation to literacy development, is more important than any early introduction to features of print.

> Wells claims that 'stories have a role in education that goes far beyond their contribution to the acquisition of literacy' (Wells 1986: 194). As I noted earlier, Tough found that retelling stories in a meaningful context was a rich source of language interaction in young children. Consult more recent sources to check whether this point is still made by researchers (see for example Hall *et al.* 2003).

In *The Meaning Makers*, Wells develops in the greatest detail the implications of the research for education (Wells 1986). If, however, you are interested in the full details of the sample selection, the language sampling and analysis and the linguistic analysis of the language, then it is to the publication *Language Development in the Preschool Years* that one must turn (Wells 1985).

Implications for early education

Of some importance is the fact that in the mid-1970s in this sample from Bristol a number of children were already attending either nursery school (or class) or a playgroup (or both) by the age of 3 years 6 months. At the time of interview this was already as high as 81 per cent, although it is stated that: 'few of the children in the younger age-range were attending nursery school at the time of interview. However, the proportion increased as the children grew older' (Wells 1985: 290). In the various publications, little further reference is made to how many children in the full sample had attended nursery school or class or playgroup before entering school, or how many of those in the longitudinal study to 10 years of age had preschool education experience. Careful reading of the many publications has revealed only passing reference. It is briefly referred to as not being associated with attainment at 7 years of age, but suggested that those already judged to be educationally at risk at 3 years of age might have been given priority admission to nursery school or class. The absence of detail on this aspect is all the more surprising in view of the detail in all other aspects. Reference is made to checking whether the child attends nursery school or playgroup, and if so, on what days, to determine appropriate days for recording.

> Since most of these children did attend preschool units it is legitimate to wonder to what extent these preschool educational experiences supported the home developments and whether they reinforced the differences already apparent; also how many of the children described in detail in case studies did attend preschool units? It is not possible to determine from this research the effects of

preschool attendance on language development. Evidence on this has recently been published from the EPPE longitudinal research (see Chapter 6).

It is a matter of concern that in the book entitled *Language Development in the Preschool Years* (Wells 1985) the 'school', to which reference is made there and repeatedly in the later reports of the longitudinal research, is the infant school entered about 5 years of age, which is studied in detail with classroom observation over the children's first 2 years in school. It was logical to seek funding and to gain extensive funds to utilize such detailed language samples and to obtain information for these children after entry to primary school, which could then be compared and contrasted with their day at home (see Wells 1986, ch. 5). What is disturbing is the tenor of a number of the comments, which might suggest to readers that for all or most of these children entry to infant school was their first experience of education outside the home. Clearly, even from the limited information given, this was not the case. The dialogue of Gary in the home (Wells 1986: 71–78) for example clearly owed something to stimulus in the nursery school (or class), yet only passing reference to this attendance is made to explain topics under discussion. Reference is made only in passing to Rosie's prior attendance at nursery class: 'a few weeks after this recording, Rosie started school. Although she had been attending a nursery class, this was her first experience of formal schooling' (Wells, 1986: 96). Indeed all but three of the group of 32 children followed into school had previously attended some form of preschool unit (I found this out in response to a question I asked Gordon Wells during an interview in Toronto in the mid-1980s).

A number of quotations that refer to infant school could give the impression that was the child's first school, or even, as in the quotation below, that it was preschool which was studied in this research:

> As with other researchers who had compared the language experiences of younger children at home and in the nursery or preschool playgroup, what we found is that compared with homes, schools are not providing an environment that fosters language development.

> (Wells 1986: 87)

Wells states that even the most linguistically deprived children in his study did not have language experience in the classroom that was richer than that of the home (note: he is referring to classrooms in infant schools). He compares his findings in this connection with those of Tizard from her study of young preschool girls at home and at nursery schools and classes (to be discussed below). Based on the classroom observations in the infant school Wells gives examples of how this affects the children's responses. The in-service materials and courses that Tough developed raised the awareness of many teachers about young children's ability to communicate given a variety of contexts, appropriate materials and skilled probing by a genuinely interested enquirer. Wells gives further important pointers about effective communication, both between child and adult and between adult and child. It is interesting to note that the transcripts from this study were later made available to others, including Aubrey and her colleagues, who were able to study children's early numeracy experiences at home (Aubrey, Godfrey and Godfrey 2000). Unfortunately the transcripts are no longer available.

What insights about the language of young children can be deduced from this longitudinal study by Wells? Note that what limitations there are are consequences of the sampling and methods.

LANGUAGE AT HOME AND AT PRESCHOOL: TIZARD AND HUGHES

This study was funded by SSRC in the later years of the 1970s. The most widely cited report of the research findings from home and school is Tizard and Hughes 1984 (a new edition was published in 2002). A number of papers based on the study were already in print much earlier in academic journals:

- Tizard et al. 1980: focused on contrasts between the language of the young children when talking with mothers and when talking with teachers
- Tizard et al. 1982: focused on adults' cognitive demands in the two settings
- Tizard et al. 1983a: reported the children's questions and adults answers
- Tizard et al. 1983b: discussed, under the title 'Language and social class: is verbal deprivation a myth?', the issues raised earlier on 'verbal deprivation' in the context of the research findings.

These topics are also covered in a more narrative style in Tizard and Hughes 1984. Tizard and Hughes challenge the formulations about disadvantage in the home and the need to teach working-class parents how to talk with their children, as some interpreted the earlier findings of Tough. Their findings with regard to the home as a language context are linked to and shown to support those of Wells (discussed earlier) and those of Davie and of John and Corinne Hutt (to follow).

The research by Tizard and Hughes is based on recordings with a radio microphone of naturally occurring dialogue of girls with staff at preschool in the morning and at home with their mothers in the afternoon. These recordings over several sessions of about two-and-a-half hours were then transcribed and analysed.

The publication usually cited in reference lists for students is *Young Children Learning* (Tizard and Hughes 1984, second edition 2002). As that publication does not give sufficient detail to allow a critical evaluation of the research, this chapter gives full details of the other publications, as cited in Clark (1988).

The sample

This study was of 30 girls of about 4 years of age. Half the girls were working-class (with fathers who were working-class and mothers who left school at the minimum age with no educational qualifications); half were middle-class (with fathers in professional or managerial positions and mothers who have completed or had qualified for tertiary education). The other selection criteria were that the children should attend nursery school or class in the morning and spend the afternoon at home with their mothers. The children from the two social classes were drawn from the same nine nursery schools and classes in two local education authorities (LEAs). Where more than two children fulfilled the criteria, selection was random. All schools and parents agreed to take part in the study, which involved recording and the presence of an observer at home in the afternoons as well as recording in the nursery school. Three mornings at school and two afternoons at home were recorded; in each case the first day's recording was discarded. The recording at home that was analysed covered the early part of afternoon (1–3.30 p.m.), that at school covered two mornings (9–11.30 a.m.) (excluding any formal story or music sessions for the whole group). Children's talk with other children at school was recorded but not analysed. Only two girls selected refused to co-operate and were thus replaced by two others.

The following were excluded:

- boys
- children not attending part-time preschool education
- children not at home with their mothers in the afternoon (thus any whose mothers worked full-time)
- children whose father was at home in the afternoon
- children who came from families with more than three children
- children in homes where the main language spoken was not English.

In short, to quote Tizard *et al.*:

> The working-class children in our study could not in any reasonable sense be considered 'deprived'; they lived in small, two-parent families, the majority in council housing, and appeared to be well cared for, much loved, and plentifully supplied with toys. Since nursery schooling in Britain, although free, is not compulsory, it is possible that they came from particularly caring, or educationally orientated families. At any rate, they

were probably typical of the majority of working-class children who attend half-day nursery school, and who are nevertheless seen by their teachers as in need of language enrichment.

(Tizard *et al.* 1980: 52)

Thus this study was similar to that of Tough in having two groups, one middle-class and one working-class, and contrasted with Tough but was similar to Wells in analysing naturally occurring language: Tizard with an observer present, Wells without; both by means of a radio microphone. Like Wells, Tizard recorded at home and at school. However, Tizard undertook those recordings concurrently; Wells had no information on the language of his group in the preschool unit, but recorded in infant school at a later stage. Tizard's sample was aged about 4 years, while Tough's sample was initially aged 3 years of age, but highly selective. Unfortunately Tizard and Hughes, in their much quoted book, seldom make reference to the fact that their sample was all girls, using the word children in the title *Young Children Learning* and on almost every occasion in the book (although of course girls' names are used throughout) (Tizard and Hughes 1984).

> Many people who have read about the research only in that book have admitted to failing to appreciate that the sample was of girls only. Consider what differences there might have been in the findings had there also been a sample of boys.

Tizard and Hughes indicate how similar to the findings of Wells theirs are in showing extended and complex conversations in the homes. In the Tizard and Hughes study, the sampling of language is for a shorter period but the recording is continuous, while in the Wells study it covered the day from 9 a.m. to 6 p.m. but in 90-second 'bursts', and it was also longitudinal. Unfortunately neither study is able to give evidence on dialogue at bedtime; this would have been valuable, particularly with regard to story reading. Because of their criteria both may undervalue the contribution of fathers to their children's language development (see Davie *et al.* 1984). Taken together, however, these studies gave new insights into the *contribution* of the home to the language development of young children.

The findings

Tizard and Hughes make the following points concerning the conversation, with comparisons between social classes and between home and school:

- *Number of adult–child conversations*: no social class differences in numbers were found, but there were fewer at school than at home.

- *Length of conversations*: no social class differences, but conversations at home tended to have more 'turns' than at school.
- *Who initiated*: in all settings the children initiated about half the conversations – no differences between social classes or between home and school.
- *Past and future events*: the majority of school conversations concerned play activity whereas at home a number were on a range of topics, including past and future events. There was also a social class difference with conversations, with middle-class children more often concerned with the past and future.
- *Length of conversation*: both at home and at school, much the longest conversations concerned books that the adult was reading aloud or had just read aloud and/or when engaged in a joint activity. There were more stories recorded in the working-class homes that the middle-class homes. It is suggested this was because the 'peak' story time in the latter would be evenings.
- *Numbers and type of questions*: children asked many questions at home, few at school, with no social class difference. The number was highest in relation to books and past and future events. At home and school, middle-class children, however, asked a higher proportion of 'non-specific' why and how questions, and the proportion for both classes was higher at home.
- *Adult responses*: proportion of 'elaborate' answers was higher at school, and both at home and at school middle-class children received more elaborate answers.
- *Relationship between child's conversation at home and school*: correlations were low and not significant, thus a child who talked a lot or asked a lot of questions at home or who tended to initiate conversation is not necessarily likely to do so at school.

All the above points are taken from Tizard *et al.* (1980: 55–68).

Finally, it should be noted that the children's intelligence was assessed at the end of the research by someone not involved in the study. The results showed a difference on a standardized test between the two social classes (the classes having been matched to be comparable on other variables, as indicated earlier): working-class girls IQ 106.4 (SD 13.2), middle-class girls 122.3 (SD 11.3). This is important since it may reflect differences in the two groups in intellectual development, or it may instead reflect the differential effect of a formalized setting with a strange adult on the young girls in the two groups. This relates to points made by Tough (1977) concerning her two groups of children, whose IQ changed differentially (and Davie *et al.* 1984).

Such findings raise the possibility that the level of language competence of 'working-class' children may well be underestimated in such situations and in other formal situations. This may result in adults providing less-challenging dialogue with some children than they have potential to sustain, and may indeed show in other naturalistic settings.

Tizard and Hughes do discuss the relationship between IQ and other factors of language, showing that there was a tendency for the working-class children with higher IQs to talk more at school and ask more questions than those with lower IQs, a finding which could be related to the point made above (from Tizard *et al.* 1980: 55–68 and Tizard and Hughes 1984).

The comparisons between language at home and at school by Tizard and Hughes have been considered in this chapter rather than Chapter 6 although they have relevance to the topic discussed there. In the preschools, Tizard and Hughes considered only the language of the girls in the free-play setting with the adults (teachers and others); dialogue with other children was *not* analysed. It is possible that other settings planned by the adults might have been a stimulus to language, as well as to social interaction. (See Chapter 8 for evidence from peer interaction in educational settings.) Tizard and Hughes take little account of the possibility that the attendance at a preschool each morning by each girl in their sample might have influenced either the content of the language in the afternoons or the readiness of the mother to indulge in such extended dialogue over a period of time.

You should consider the following points:
- How different would the evidence have been had these girls not attended preschool in the mornings?
- Had the sample included boys at home in the afternoons, would the social class patterns indeed have been the same and the home/school differences been the same, less or greater?
- Would a comparable sample of young girls not attending nursery school have given similar results at home? Indeed, would there have been some mothers in such a sample who would not have agreed to participate?

In Tizard and Hughes (1984) there is discussion on parental attitudes and ways in which these may differ across the classes, and of subtle social class differences in line with some of the points made earlier by Tough. To quote one example:

We found that the middle-class mothers used language for complex purposes significantly more often than the working-class mothers – on average, adding the different usages together, fifty-one times an hour compared with thirty-eight times an hour for working-class mothers. The proportion, as well as the rate, of these uses of language was higher in the talk of the middle-class mothers. The averages conceal wide variations and there was a good deal of overlap between the social classes.

(Tizard and Hughes 1984: 141)

> Consider the relationship between mothers' views of their own contribution to their child's development and the dialogue in which they engage. The assumption current in the early 1970s of deprivation of language and deficiencies in homes could well have reinforced attitudes of incompetence in parents such as the 'working-class' mothers in this study.

A discussion of such attitudes in parents from a much more 'deprived' section of the community than were involved in these studies, and of ways in which not only their attitudes but also those of their children's teachers to the parents' contributions might be modified, is reported by Donachy (1976 and 1979).

> Now that you have read more detail on the research by Tizard and Hughes than you would obtain in Tizard and Hughes 1984 or 2002, it would be valuable to note the strengths and weaknesses of the research. Check what claims are made for it in many of the citations in textbooks. How many of these claims do you now feel are justified?

EXPERIENCES AT HOME: DAVIE, S. J. AND C. HUTT AND OTHERS

The parallel studies of 'the young child's experiences at home' and of 'play, exploration and learning in the preschool' directed by John and Corinne Hutt at the University of Keele were among the first researches to be funded by DES within the programme of research on preschool education in 1970s. The empirical work for both was undertaken in the 1970s. The report of the research on experiences in the home, published as *The Young Child at Home*, is the source for the evidence discussed here (Davie *et al.* 1984). The parallel study in preschool units became the responsibility of John Hutt after Corinne Hutt's death. Supporting evidence from the research in the preschool units is cited by Davie and Hutt in the book referred to above. The research in preschool units was later published as *Play, Exploration and Learning* (Hutt *et al.* 1989). Attention will be confined here to the study in the homes because the parallel study did not involve the same sample children (see Chapter 6 for their studies in preschool units).

The sample

This study was of 165 children living in Stoke-on-Trent and the immediately surrounding area. The sample was balanced for sex (boys and girls), age (3–3.5,

3.5–4, 4–4.5 years) and family position (eldest, only, youngest). Documentation available locally was used for initial approaches to large numbers of families, with assistance from local personnel to obtain a representative sample (as in Wells' study). Details are given in Davie *et al.* (1984: ch. 2) of sample selection and of possible bias as a result of families that were unwilling or unable to co-operate.

Children were excluded who:

- had any serious health defect
- were not of United Kingdom or Irish origin
- were from single-parent families
- were attending nursery school or class, a day nursery or a playgroup for more than two sessions per week.

The following points are noted with regard to the sample of children and their families (see Davie *et al.* 1984: ch. 3):

- About half the sample (of both classes) lived in 'semidetached' houses.
- Most of the middle-class parents and a high proportion of the working-class parents were owner-occupiers (there were cheap terraced houses for sale), almost a third of the working-class were in council accommodation.
- Few lived in flats, and where they did it was on the first floor (it was the city's declared policy not to house families with small children in high-rise apartments).
- All families had sole use of toilet facilities (although in a few old properties the toilet might be outside).
- Overcrowding was not a problem.
- Only one family had no outside area that was their own.
- Few were living adjacent to very busy roads.
- The majority were car owners (with a social class difference).
- All families had television sets.
- All but four fathers were working.
- Few mothers worked full-time, but 39 per cent were working (more middle-class than working-class).
- Fathers or relations tended to be caretaker when the mother worked, although a few went to a childminder.
- Most of the families had close relatives in the area (both maternal and paternal).

The findings

Like Wells and Tizard, Davie and colleagues studied the young children in natural settings in the home. However, unlike the previous researchers, they extended their study in time to the child's waking hours and in space to beyond the house. Like Tizard (but not Wells) they had an observer, and also attempted to assess and minimize observer effects. Unlike Tizard and Wells they did not record language by use of a radio microphone; they did, however, categorize language interactions and devote a chapter to language.

This study gives a picture of the experiences at play and interactions with parents, siblings and relatives over the equivalent of a day, sampled in 2-hour blocks over several days, for a group of normal preschool boys and girls. Thus the relative pattern of experiences over the day of boys and girls is studied, and their interactions with both mother and father are considered. Lacking are full transcripts of the content of the dialogue, which could be reanalysed by others, as was possible with the language from Wells' study. Details of the observational schedule are provided in their appendix. As in the other researches discussed here, social class was a major concern because it was felt that 'so much attention has been paid to it in earlier research, using different techniques and the findings from this research have affected the attitudes of people concerned with the education of the young child' (Davie *et al.* 1984: 177).

> From their evidence Davie *et al.* claim that social class does not operate as strongly as has been suggested. They found that the vast majority of the children in their sample had plenty of toys and that working-class parents spent as much time talking and interacting with their children as did middle-class parents. They note that the differences they found were subtle and qualitative. Compare these findings with the other researches discussed so far and consider what might have caused the differences they found.

Middle-class parents were more inclined to provide toys of so-called 'educational value', their children had more plentiful supplies of books and were encouraged to spend time on activities more related to developing the beginning of academic skills. On the completion of the observation period the children were assessed by the observer on the Stanford Binet Intelligence Scale. Social class differences were found which, it was suggested, could have been related to the experience in activities such as are in these tests. A sex difference was also found, with the girls scoring higher on the test. Greater competence in language was shown by some children in the natural setting (see Davie *et al.* 1984: 151–2).

> Here again we have differences found in the natural settings and in test situation, with greater competence shown in the natural settings. Furthermore, the comments below are in line with the more recent findings of Hart and Risley (1995).

Like Wells, these researchers observed that 'abstract' explanations were rare, even by middle-class parents. They do suggest, however, that there were subtle and qualitative differences in language usage of parents to their children. For example, there was more use by some of the working-class parents of 'instructions', which were redundant as the child already knew the labels. In contrast, the novelty of the 'instructions' from some of the middle-class parents 'appeared to stimulate their children to demand more "instructions"' (Davie *et al*. 1984: 178). Both groups used what they categorized as 'options' as effective ways of controlling their children; that is, suggestions or invitations to take part in a new activity or to deflect from a less acceptable one. It is claimed that options and also praise were more frequently used by middle-class parents. Middle-class children were also receiving more options from peers, suggesting 'that older siblings were developing similar tactics to their parents towards their siblings' (Davie *et al*. 1984: 149). Their categorizations of speech were based on the work of Bernstein (Davie *et al*. 1984: 148). Speech was 'categorized' rather than recorded, and the researchers note that very subtle differences in language production could not be revealed in their study (Davie *et al*. 1984: 136).

Because of the balanced sample it was possible to study a more complex pattern of variables, not only social class but also sex differences, if any, and the effect of position in the family on interaction with adults and young children. It was found for example that there were differences between boys and girls not only in their toys but also in their preferred activities and types of fantasy play; this was also found in free play in nursery schools. Position in family strongly influenced interaction with adults and children: 'oldest' children were more like 'only' children, 'youngest' children interacted less with adults and more with children. There was no evidence of differential interactions of mother and fathers with young sons and daughters, even in rough-and-tumble play, although fathers were more inclined to play football with sons. Fathers were less inclined to interact with youngest children. Girls neither spoke more nor received more general or particular forms of speech, although they did score higher on the intelligence test.

> This is one of the few studies where the differences between boys and girls in their interactions is considered, and the plan of the research allows the role of the father to be fully investigated. I wonder how many others you can find where 'parent' does not just mean mother!

Implications for early education

The published report does contain sufficient detail on a number of points for replication to be possible, including details of the observation schedule. Where differences between groups were found, it would have been helpful to have known how much overlap there was between groups, particularly where comments were made on social class differences. Details are given concerning the social and physical environments of the area and of the children in the two social classes, something not provided in sufficient detail by some research workers. A summary will be given of the features of the environment detailed by the researchers to help you in assessing the generalizability of their study.

The following points are noted with regard to the area in which the study took place (see Davie *et al.* 1984: ch. 3 and p. 160):

- The children all lived in or near Stoke-on-Trent (thus were urban).
- The employment in the area is in the potteries and mining, and also in a large tyre factory (influencing patterns of employment, including of females).
- The area has many parks.
- The city has a history of early provision of preschool education, with nursery schools and classes, also day nurseries, already provided by the 1970s.
- Provision of preschool education was increased because of women's employment in the potteries.
- Nursery school attendance was normally full-time.

The above points would all need to be considered in any attempt to replicate the study or to compare the findings with other more recent studies.

The chapter they devote to preschool provision and parents' attitudes to preschool provision is based in part on the wider sample of over a thousand families contacted initially. Parents were shown to be confused about the nature of different types of provision for young children. The reason for sending children to a playgroup or nursery school most frequently cited was to mix with other children. More middle-class than working-class parents in the sample were in favour of keeping their child at home, for child-centred reasons, especially where nursery school was concerned (it is noted that attendance was normally full-time). Middle-class parents in the sample were more likely than working-class parents to give 'developmental' reasons for wanting their children to attend playgroup. About half of the sample attended playgroup at the time of initial contact and there was a highly significant class difference, with many more middle-class than working-class children attending.

> You will find other researches, including the recent EPPE study (Sylva *et al.* 2004a; 2004b), also show that parents may have very different reasons for sending their children to a preschool unit, and that some may make a conscious decision to keep their child at home. The children in the EPPE research were 3 years of age in 1997, so by then there would have been much more preschool education available than at the time of this research (final report of EPPE research, Sylva *et al.* 2004a).

As may be appreciated, the conditions of the families in this research are very different from the multiple deprivation from which other families may suffer. They may live in overcrowded conditions in high-rise flats, near to busy roads, with no outside play area, a low income or unemployment and with no relatives in the area. Some children may in addition to all the above be from single-parent families, and with very young mothers. It is important to consider the environment in which these children live and all the constraints the environment places on parental interaction with their children, and between siblings. There is growing evidence of the depression of many young mothers in these circumstances and its effect on the children in the home, and the parent's inability to take advantage of preschool facilities which may be available (Shinman 1981).

This study illustrates how some patterns of interaction might plausibly be explained by differences between home environments, rather than by differences in preferred styles of child-rearing between classes (to which they may be attributed by some researchers). It is essential that multiple deprivation and poverty are not confused with social class influences, a point well made by these researchers.

This study by Davie and the Hutts is rich in insights into the lives of these 165 preschool children within their extended families. Its plan and the amount of day covered makes it one of the few studies in which the relative interactions of mothers and fathers is studied in relation also to the sex of the children and their positions in their families. The activities and interactions available to these young preschool children are shown to be wide and varied. Any differences related to social class are at most 'subtle and qualitative'. Social class differences may be widened in 'contrived' and experimental settings which may have differential effects on parents and children from different social classes. In relation to the contexts in preschool units they suggest that:

> the preschool setting may have a similar effect, constraining and inhibiting the young working-class child, so that, for example, his speech and fantasy play are curtailed, enhancing differences that are not apparent at home.

(Davie et al. 1984: 178)

This observation is supported by the evidence from Tizard and Hughes' study on the differential effects of school on the social classes, with the middle-class children displaying a competence in school more similar to that at home. This is certainly not a situation peculiar to the preschool unit. As shown by Wells and other researchers, it might also be true in primary schools. Do you think this might still be true; if not in the reception class, then at the later stages in the primary school?

FINAL COMMENTS

In view of the findings reported in this chapter on the differential effects on language of the context, of home and school and of social class, the proposal by Robinson noted in the previous chapter becomes all the more significant. He suggests that teachers predict children's attainment partly on the basis of what he refers to as 'the language management of children'; that they overestimate the size of the correlation between social class, speech and academic potential and that the 'differentials are communicated to and perceived by the children' (Robinson 1980: 38–9).

Do you feel that many teachers are still influenced by the factors considered here and that their judgements do influence children's self-esteem?

AN ANALYSIS OF A RESEARCH ON THE LANGUAGE OF CHILDREN UNDER 3 YEARS IN THEIR HOMES

In the previous chapter I referred to a longitudinal study of American children, which is currently receiving a great deal of publicity on both sides of the Atlantic, and further publications are anticipated. I have read carefully through the publication, *Meaningful Differences in the Everyday Experience of Young American Children* (Hart and Risley 1995), which is based on observations of children in their homes over 2 years until they were 3 years of age and a follow up of some of the sample through their elementary school. My focus in the present book is on a critical analysis of researches undertaken in United Kingdom, although linking these with developments in the United States. Rather than presenting a critical evaluation of Hart and Risley's research, I would prefer to set you the challenge of making such an analysis yourself and comparing it with the studies that have been discussed in this chapter. One point that is worth drawing to your attention is the date of the commencement of Hart and Risley's research; this I tracked down as 1983, which is therefore nearly contemporary with some of the research discussed in this chapter. In the previous chapter I set out a framework that should help you evaluate this and other recent studies.

Section II

Research in preschool units: what lessons can we learn?

Chapter 4

Studies in preschool units: researches in the 1970s and 1980s set in context

FRAMEWORK FOR EVALUATION

I will start this section by providing you with a framework from which to evaluate any research into preschool education; indeed many of the points apply to any evaluation of educational initiatives. You may think of other points.

- *The timescale of the empirical work should be stated.* It is not sufficient to note the date of publication of the research because in a number of instances some time elapses between its completion and the appearance of the published version.
- *The area or areas in which the research was undertaken should be clearly indicated.* Some background information should be given on the part of the United Kingdom or other country in which it took place; if the area is within only one LEA, its policy for preschool provision needs to be known. Where only 5 per cent of those under 5 years of age attend preschool units; or where many children aged between 4 and 5 years are already in infant school reception classes, the samples would not be comparable.
- *The precise type of preschool units in which the research took place should be stated.* If this is not stated, it is impossible to compare findings.
- *The nature of the staffing in the unit should be indicated.* Not only the adult : child ratio, but also how many of the adults are qualified, and whether they are teachers, nursery nurses or parents. In some units there may be qualified teachers, in others only one teacher and the remaining staff are nursery nurses, in others only nursery nurses or other practitioners.
- *The age range of the children needs to be indicated, and how long before entry to primary school they attended the preschool unit.* You will see from the research discussed in chapters 8 and 9, which took place in only five schools, just how different the age ranges of children entering reception class can be.

- *The amount of parental involvement in the unit is important.* It is also important to know what is the nature of the involvement of those parents who do attend.
- *Whether the children in the study attend more than one preschool unit, either concurrently or consecutively, may well be of significance.* This information is seldom stated in research.
- *The number of hours per week the children attend is another important variable.* Some children only attend for a few hours per week, while at the other extreme children may attend full-time, or even for an extended day.

SETTING THE SCENE

Chapters 5 and 6 are devoted to a discussion of several of the funded researches in preschool units that took place in the 1970s and 1980s and which are still cited on reference lists. Researches in the first newly opened nursery schools in Dunbartonshire in Scotland will be discussed in Chapter 5. These collaborative studies, undertaken in consultation with the head teachers and funded jointly by Dunbartonshire and the Scottish Education Department (SED), were reported in *Studies in Preschool Education* (Clark and Cheyne 1979).

Chapter 6 will analyse two researches in preschool units in England funded within the SSRC/DES Programme in anticipation of the proposed expansion of preschool education in the 1970s. This is a modified version of Chapter 7 in *Children Under Five* (Clark 1988). Unfortunately, while the researches were still underway the expansion ceased and there were threats of closure of a number of nursery schools; this made some settings less willing to welcome researchers who were casting a critical eye on their practice.

Finally I will consider the implications of the longitudinal research on the effectiveness of preschool education, EPPE, funded by DfES between 1997 and 2003, the final report appeared as I completed this book. The aims of that study were to assess the effects of preschool education on children's development, differences in outcome between different types of setting, and more specifically to identify the characteristics of the good settings (Sylva *et al.* 2004a).

The evidence from the 1970s and 1980s shows how varied was the provision of preschool services across the country, how little co-operation there was between services or co-ordination of services (see Clark 1988). Some LEAs gave priority within their budgets to building nursery schools or opening nursery classes attached to primary schools, often in more-deprived areas. Some authorities already provided for over 50 per cent, others had fewer than 5 per cent attending nursery school or classes. Furthermore some LEAs had no nursery schools, and others only a few or no nursery classes. In some areas where research was undertaken there was already provision in a nursery school or class for all those children whose parents wished them to attend, particularly in some very deprived inner-city areas. In addition, in England by

1985 there had been a marked increase in the total number of children under 5 years of age in infant classes in primary school, here also with wide differences between LEAs. Some LEAs, by admitting children only just 4 years of age to reception class, provided a less-expensive form of education than in conventional preschool units; however, the staff : child ratio, and even the facilities, were in no way comparable. This development was criticized, and continues to be, by many researchers as providing inferior early education.

There was wide variation across the United Kingdom in whether there was any available preschool education, in the types of preschool unit, for how many sessions the children could attend and the precise age at which children entered primary school (although, as currently in the United Kingdom, it was around 5 years of age, and much earlier than in most other countries). In other areas, preschool playgroups established by groups of parents, providing only a few sessions per week and not held in purpose-built settings, were the only places available.

> Note that the term 'playgroup' is often used in research and elsewhere as if it refers to a specific type of provision; it might actually be used to cover a variety of provision, attracting children from very different backgrounds. Some playgroups might be attended by middle-class families, others might be provided for disadvantaged families.

Some playgroups were self-help groups set up by mothers within which they themselves helped, which they organized and for which they provided funds; others received public funds and were staffed by voluntary agencies and had qualified staff.

In the 1970s and 1980s a few LEAs began to develop combined nursery centres to provide preschool education and day care in a single unit; in several cases they were established as a result of joint applications by education and social services for Urban Aid funds. Pen Green Centre in Corby, still a focus for innovative research and development projects, was opened in 1983. Clearly such units were likely to meet a considerable challenge and many problems in bringing together in a joint venture two services with separate administrative and professional settings.

For young working parents requiring full day care for their children from an early age, there were day nurseries, some funded by LEAs; though there were not nearly sufficient of these.

Alternatively childminders, who cared for groups of young children in the childminder's home, might be the only available resource (see chapters 8 and 9 in Clark 1988 for a discussion of research on combined centres, day nurseries and of childminders).

In short, some parents were lucky enough to have access for their children to free places in a custom-built nursery school, or nursery class attached to a primary school, at least half-day; others were able to enrol their children in a preschool playgroup for a few hours a week, many of which expected the parents not only to pay for their child's attendance, but also to spend some time there themselves. Still other children were from a very early age in a private or local-authority-funded day nursery, or with a childminder paid for by the parents. Many parents, particularly those living in rural areas, had no access to preschool education for their children.

> I suggest you make a list of background features you need to consider if you are to compare the findings from researches conducted in different areas, in different types of units, or at different times. You need to consider not only features of the units, but also information on the home background of the children. As you will see from the recently completed EPPE research, the family and child characteristics differ widely for different types of provision, making comparison between types of unit a very complex statistical exercise (see Chapter 6).

The researches I will discuss in the following chapters took place in a variety of settings; however, parents seldom had a choice of which type of provision their child could attend, or for how many sessions. Even where there is extensive provision of preschool services, if attendance is not compulsory, some parents will still choose not to send their children because of cost, distance to the nearest unit, unsuitability of available times, or even their beliefs about what is provided within preschool units.

RECENT DEVELOPMENTS

This is not the place to track the changes in preschool provision over the years since its introduction. There are some common themes in the development of early education in the constituent parts of the United Kingdom over recent years which contrast with the 1970s and 1980s. Free preschool education is now available for 3- and 4-year-olds whose parents wish them to attend (though it is still not compulsory). However, the recent EPPE study has provided evidence that there are currently children who do not attend a preschool unit and so enter primary school direct from home, some for the kinds of reasons mentioned above (Sammons *et al.* 2004). Curriculum guidelines for the children aged 3 to 5 years now reflect many of the aims of early educators; for example, in Scotland *Curriculum Framework for Children 3 to 5* (SCCC 1999), and in England *Curriculum Guidance for the Foundation Stage* (QCA/DfEE 2000). Currently, in England the Foundation Stage refers only to children up to the age of 5 years, though this is likely to be extended. In Wales, according to the Minister for Lifelong Learning, integrated centres will be established in all LEAs and 'the new innovative and uniquely Welsh proposals for a Foundation Phase for three–seven year olds are profound and far reaching' (Davidson 2004: 4). The Scottish Executive is now considering revision to the national guidelines (currently 5–14, but linked with the 3–5 guidelines) to cover the age range 3–18 years. Attention has now turned to the needs of children under 3 years of age, with in England *Birth to Three Matters: a framework to support children in their earliest years* (DfES/Sure Start 2002), and in Scotland *Birth to Three: supporting our youngest children* (LTS 2005).

In the United Kingdom there are many government initiatives in early education; these involve massive increase in funding, additional staffing and schemes to improve the qualifications of those concerned with the education and care of young children, and curricular guidelines for early education (see Pugh 2001 and the various government websites). While there is still an emphasis on provision for those in greatest need, many of the current initiatives are directed to supporting families, particularly to supporting young mothers who need help in bringing up their families, and also help to enable them to enter the workforce or gain qualifications. Currently, not only in the United Kingdom but also in many other countries, there is an emphasis on co-ordination of education and care, with the term 'educare' signalling this; inspection of preschool services now involves co-operation between educational and social services. Wrap-around care based in schools, to provide for children both before and after school should their parents' work require this, is a further initiative.

Contrary to what you may read in many publications, although there are similarities in recent developments over the constituent parts of the United Kingdom, including Sure Start, there are also differences, particularly in terminology. While the terms 'Foundation Stage' and 'Foundation Stage Profile', 'reception class', 'Key Stages', 'SATs' and the 'National Curriculum' all apply in England, none of them apply in Scotland (see Clark and Munn 1997; Bryce and Humes 2003). Furthermore, the age of admission to primary school is different in Scotland, with children entering Primary 1 (the first class in primary school, not the reception class) at the beginning of the school year if they will be 5 years of age by the end of February. In contrast, in England the oldest children entering reception class will be in the term after their fifth birthday, the youngest at the beginning of the school year when they are just 4 years of age, with wide differences even in neighbouring LEAs. As I noted in Chapter 1, DfES is responsible for education and care within England only, education in Scotland and Wales is the responsibility of the Scottish Parliament and Welsh Assembly, respectively. Curricular materials and documents for England come from the QCA; those for Scotland from Learning and Teaching Scotland, which issues a twice yearly newsletter entitled *Early Years' Matters*.

AIMS IN EARLY EDUCATION

As I stated in Chapter 2, language improvement was one justification expressed for the expansion of preschool education in 1970s, with a belief that experience in a preschool setting, with free play and contact with professional adults, would be sufficient to bridge the gap between home and infant school. Not many preschools in the United Kingdom introduced specific language programmes, such as were introduced in the United States. Observational studies in preschool units with a focus on target children, such as those to be discussed in the following chapters, revealed that in many settings the free play context, with a wide choice of activities available simultaneously, did not necessarily provide a cognitively stimulating programme, nor much extended dialogue between the professionals and those children in greatest need. It should be remembered, however, that for many practitioners language was not *their* first priority. Many teachers and assistants saw social development as the first priority, followed by more-specifically educational aims, such as preparation for school. Many parents sending their children to preschool might also give greater priority to social development, learning to mix with others or preparation for school.

> What many parents believed took place in preschool units was often not in accord with the aims of the staff, or indeed the practice in such settings. Many staff in the primary schools to which those children who attended preschool units would proceed were also not aware of the aims or practices of the preschool settings. This may still be true. You might find it valuable to explore the perceptions of staff in a primary school concerning the aims and curriculum of preschool settings.

The need to assist the language development of young children, particularly those from so-called 'disadvantaged homes' whose language was thought not to be adequate for the cognitive demands of schooling (a common theme in the 1970s), is still a matter of concern. There are many articles deploring the limited vocabulary and inarticulateness of young children entering primary school. Lack of conversation in the homes and the negative effects of indiscriminate or unsupervised television viewing on the vocabulary of very young children are among the topics being investigated (see Close 2004 for a review of the research literature). The National Literacy Trust was responsible for the literature search on television viewing and launched a project in 2003 entitled 'Talk to Your Baby' (see www.literacytrust.org.uk). See also the recently published book *Popular Culture, New Media and Digital Literacy in Early Childhood* (Marsh 2005). Polly Toynbee in the article referred to in Chapter 2, based on the findings of an American study by Hart and Risley (1995), makes a justification for preschool education similar to that made in the 1970s and 1980s (Toynbee 2004). She argues that if we wish to change 'class destiny' it will take good teachers in high-quality children's centres, where children of all classes mix, not only the deprived together; only then will we make good what is still being seen as deficient or impoverished language. When formal schooling starts, she argues, it is too late. For that reason alone it is worth considering what lessons we can learn from the researches in preschool units in the 1970s and 1980s.

I hope you now appreciate the need to ensure that you are aware of the historical setting within which any researches are undertaken, and that this applies to comparative studies in different countries as much as to past and current researches within a single country.

Chapter 5

Studies of preschool education in Scotland

Lessons from the past

OUTLINE OF THE PROJECTS

In this chapter I will discuss a series of projects in preschool units in Scotland undertaken during the early 1970s. These have received less publicity than those in England; yet they are significant, particularly because of their collaborative nature, not common at that time. A local authority in Scotland, Dunbartonshire, invited me to undertake research on their developing nursery education; this they funded jointly with the Scottish Education Department (SED). The first school opened in 1970, quickly followed by four other schools on the same open plan, and a nursery class attached to a primary school, all in areas of multiple deprivation. Each school as it was opened joined the project. Our studies developed partly from the ideas of the researchers and partly from our meetings with the head teachers, whom we encouraged to raise issues about nursery education and topics they would like us to investigate. Rather than a single large project we undertook a number of smaller studies, some of which were published as articles; all, including an associated parental participation study in another county, are reported in *Studies in Preschool Education* (Clark and Cheyne 1979).

By working in close collaboration with the staff we were able to provide them with insights, leading them on occasion to modify their practice. We helped them develop written records for training staff, and encouraged and supported them in their observation of individual children, helping them to appreciate the differences in children's apparent language competence in a variety of settings, including during tests. We were not seen as a threat, as were some researchers at that time, rather as a support to practitioners, many of who were new to working in preschool education. As a consequence of the information from our observations in some instances they reconsidered the available choices of activities and the placement of adults within the nursery to ensure that all children had a range of experiences during their time there. Not only were we able to observe children at a given point in time, we were also able to observe some children over their 2 years in nursery, comparing the choices of activities of the boys and girls, and of older and younger children. At that time parents did not tend to be present in the nursery schools; indeed the design of the new nursery schools made it very difficult for head teachers who did wish to encourage parents to be present. One head teacher, aware of the value of involving the parents, appealed for funds for an extension to provide space for parents.

I obtained secondment for an educational psychologist, Bill Donachy, who was working with very disadvantaged parents and their preschool children in a neighbouring county; this enabled him to join our team and extend his research. His pioneering work attracted a great deal of attention, and later when he moved to Northern Ireland he was able to introduce his ideas when working with parents and young children there also. His programme included lending books to the parents of preschool children, these they were encouraged to share with their young children. They were given supportive materials and also met for informal discussions with other mothers in the primary school that their children would soon attend. Initially Donachy supplied toys, but found that books stimulated better discussion. Through co-operation from health visitors he had been able to include 'hard to reach' parents whose children were unlikely to have attended preschool education. His extended project was a balanced experimental design, with control groups, nursery and non-nursery children with and without the programme. In order to assess any effects on the children he used a number of standardized language tests. Not only were there significant effects on the children's development after an intervention of 4 months, but also the project raised the self-esteem of these mothers and changed the attitude of some of the teachers in the primary school to these families (Donachy 1976 and 1979).

I appreciate how much nursery education has changed over the intervening years, and the wealth of research that is now available. I have therefore selected only one of our projects to discuss here, that of interest in books and stories in children attending one of the nursery schools in which we worked.

It has become increasingly common to assess young children either in preschool settings or shortly after their entry to primary school, and for a variety of purposes. I am sure you will be able to think of many such assessments. Many of the judgements made and assumptions of reliability of the measures in the settings in which they take place are overstated, even on occasion naïve. During these researches we assessed young children in many different ways, and as we did so we became aware of the many problems in making reliable assessments of young children. The second part of this chapter discusses the insights we gained during this research.

The decisions we made and our approach may give you ideas for similar studies concerning interest in books and stories or early literacy activities. I hope this chapter will help you to appreciate the importance of a clear rationale in even a small-scale study in a single setting and the need for target children in any observations you undertake.

INTEREST IN BOOKS AND STORIES

Many preschool units in Britain, and some classes in infant departments, provide a variety of different activities simultaneously for at least part of the day and allow the children considerable freedom in choosing what they do. It may therefore be difficult to keep track of who does what and for how long. The focus for this study was one kind of activity in a nursery school, namely use of books and stories, which we related to the children's abilities, and to other activities in which they engaged both at home and at school. The head teacher of the nursery school, who had previously been in charge of the infant department in a primary school, regarded as one of her major objectives helping children to an appreciation of the written word as a preparation for later reading, an unusual emphasis in preschool units in the 1970s when this study took place. Her commitment was reflected in these activities having high priority with the children, unlike the findings of other researches at that time.

The sample

The open–plan school in which this research took place, like the others in the county, had only recently opened (with the aid of special funding) and was in a very deprived urban area. It catered for 100 children, about 40 attended each morning, another 40 each afternoon and 20 all day. The head teacher was the only teacher, the remainder of the staff were nursery nurses; for most staff this was their first post in a nursery school. Most children attended for 2 years, from age 3 to 5 years.

The research took place at a time when in Britain most of the day in preschool units was devoted to free play, with the choice of activity mainly that of the children themselves. Many of the new nursery schools, certainly in Scotland at that time, were large and open plan, thus giving the children freedom to move around throughout their half day or day in the unit. This makes it more difficult to monitor the range of activities experienced by the individual children, who may select a particular activity because of their interest in it, because their friends are there or because of the adult who happens to be supervising it. They may sample many different activities, even flit from one to another, or they may spend long periods of intense concentration at particular activities. They may extend their interests over the two years, or may stay with a limited range of experiences over the period of their attendance. Only detailed observation of selected children can show just how wide are the experiences of the individual children, and how effective is the setting, no matter how wide ranging are the opportunities provided.

Stage I: General observations

This research took place in two stages. During the first stage, one of the researchers spent two days in the school recording the activities taking place and the numbers of boys, girls and adults in each group. The second researcher spent the same two days making continuous observations of the children's behaviour in the main book area, noting the time each child entered and left the area and the kinds of activity and interactions with others while there. After a month the procedure was repeated for a further three days. Meanwhile, in order to check whether children who made little use of the book area might nevertheless use books in other parts of the nursery school, the other researcher made similar observations where books and storytelling were available elsewhere. These observations were used to select two groups of children, matched in pairs for age, sex and session they attended (morning or afternoon), who seemed to have high or low interest in books and stories. There were 14 children in each group.

We found that story telling and looking at books, taken together, were among the most commonly observed activities in the nursery school. Other evidence available at that time suggested that such activities were much less common in other preschool units.

> You might seek evidence from other observation studies on the popularity of books and stories where the children have a choice of activities, and whether sex differences were found. It would be interesting to know how much this has changed over recent years with much greater emphasis now placed on early literacy in preschool education.

The detailed observation of children in the main book area, the 'book corner', showed that some children did not visit that area, or visited only for very brief periods, while others spent at least one longish period most days. Furthermore it was the same children who used the book corner who tended to use books elsewhere. There were differences in the extent to which children in the book corner sought and received adult attention. The first stage of this study, simple in design though it was, provided interesting information on the choice of play by children over the days we observed.

Certain activities, such as gluing and cutting, went on almost continuously. Others, such as story telling, went on simultaneously in two or three areas at certain periods of the day. Story reading was one of the activities for which participation of an adult was virtually essential, but the participation of an adult, or mere presence of an adult, was associated with an increase in popularity of other activities. Where there were activities at which there was on occasion an adult present, we found the adult's presence increased the number of children attracted. This was true even at water play, in which the adult usually took no active part.

We measured not only how many children used the book corner and how frequently the same children used it, but also how long particular children remained there. There was a significant difference in the use of the book corner between boys and girls, with the girls tending to spend longer periods there than the boys; younger boys were also less likely to use the book corner. Children using the book corner preferred to hear a story of their own choice, with marked individual differences in their strategies for achieving this. Some children would leave the area immediately for another activity if not successful with a request; some would take the book with them to try to find a willing adult, or would try to persuade another adult to come to the book corner, while others would remain and try again. We saw many instances of children's desire for repetition of a favourite story and of even the younger children using 'book language' in retelling a story. The children frequently spoke to themselves or to their friends in the manner of someone reading as they looked through books. This 'pretend' reading was quite different in style and delivery from interspersed comments on the story. It was unusual to see even the younger children in the book area looking at a book the wrong way up, or going through it in the wrong direction. We even heard one child excitedly telling her friends that she was about to have a story 'without pictures'.

It should be remembered that we undertook this study in the early 1970s when few observations of young children's interactions with books in preschool settings were being published. Although these language interactions were not the main focus of the study it is worth noting just how much additional information can be gained from such qualitative observations. These observations stimulated us to record the language of the young children in a variety of settings in this and the other nursery schools, using tests and story retelling as the stimulus. We were able to show how much richer was the language of these so-called 'deprived' children depending on the setting and their desire to communicate.

Stage 2: Children with high and low interest in books

As noted earlier, from our initial observations we selected two groups of children: 14 children in the 'high interest' group and 14 matched children in the comparison 'low interest' group. In the second stage of the research each child in the 'high interest' group and the comparison group was observed continuously for 100 minutes in the middle part of the session they attended. To check the reliability of the observations both researchers simultaneously observed ten of the children (of the 28 in the group); we found the reliability to be high. The range of activities and duration at each was measured for each child. Tests were also administered to find out if the children differed in ability. Parents were interviewed about their children's play activities at home and nursery nurses were asked to complete a questionnaire about the children's activities in school, using the same categories for responses.

The comparison group children engaged in more activities than the other group, but for relatively shorter periods, and spent more time doing nothing in particular. All children in the 'high interest' group were reported to have a story at home from an adult at least once a week, and in most cases once a day; this was not so common in the comparison group.

> A study with a design such as this can provide rich and valuable information on aspects of children's interests in the nursery school and at home; what it does not allow is inferences as to the extent that experiences at home and at school influence one another. A longitudinal study that explores the children's activities at home before as well as during their time at nursery school would be necessary to shed light on any directional or causal relationships.

While we do not have such information from within this series of researches, in one of the nursery schools we did undertake a longitudinal study of children over the period of their 2 years in the nursery school. There, at the request of the head teacher, we assisted in the development of written records and the training of the nursery nurses to use these. Records were kept of the children's play activities over the 2-year period. Most of the boys were reported as showing interest in the book corner by the age of 5 years, but not at 3 years or age, most of the girls, on the other hand were showing an interest at a much earlier age. As in the study of interest in books and stories, we were able to provide the head teacher with valuable information to improve her practice. Lomax was responsible for this study and several others in the project (see Lomax 1977 and 1979). Further information on the early development of literacy is discussed in Section IV, including reference to more recent research.

LESSONS ON ASSESSMENT OF YOUNG CHILDREN

There is currently emphasis on some form of baseline assessment in a number of countries to provide a basis for information, not only on 'value-added' by the school but also on individual children's current performance. This is a matter of concern in the light of the wealth of evidence on the unreliability of assessments of the language of young children, particularly by unqualified adults, by strangers or when the assessment is based on a single instance. Lindsay and Lewis undertook an evaluation of the more than 90 accredited baseline assessment schemes used in England between 1998 and 2000, when it became a statutory requirement to undertake a baseline assessment within 7 weeks of a child starting school, at about 4–5 years of age, unless the child had previously been assessed. This has now been replaced by the Foundation Stage Profile, which requires teachers to assess children not only somewhat later, but also through ongoing learning and teaching (Lindsay and Lewis 2003). A number of the issues raised by Lindsay and Lewis, and a related one on 'the consistency of baseline assessment schemes as measures of early literacy', are still pertinent (Lindsay *et al.* 2004). The concerns expressed by Shorrocks, which are based on her evaluations of SATs (Standard Assessment Tasks), undertaken at the end of Key Stage 1 in England when the children are around 7 years of age, are important (Shorrocks 1995). There have recently been changes in the focus of SATs at Key Stage 1 in England towards greater emphasis on teacher assessment, where previously the focus was on test results; in 2002 Wales abolished SATs at Key Stage 1; in Scotland there never has been a formal assessment of children nationally at 7 years of age.

Assessment of the abilities of young children may be carried out for a variety of purposes:

- collection of normative information on groups of children
- measurement of individual differences compared with others in the group or national norms
- assessment of relative strengths and weaknesses of an individual
- diagnosis of difficulties
- determination of the next step in teaching experiences
- assessment of the effectiveness of a particular part of the nursery or other programme
- training of staff, where the assessment of individual children is a means of sensitizing them to particular aspects of development
- comparison of what an individual usually does and what they can do
- prediction of future progress
- assessment of the relationship between different aspects of development.

You may find it useful to consider into which, if any, of these categories the various assessment procedures of which you are aware fit. Do you know of any important categories I have omitted?

A large number of different types of assessment were used during the course of our researches, including standardized tests, specially designed tests, semi-structured observations and rating scales. The discussion here will focus on the problems we encountered and the advantages of each approach with young children.

Tests

In theory, tests provide an efficient way of assessing children's current levels of functioning, providing information about what they can do when pushed to their limits rather than showing what they usually do, as may be the case with observational procedures. Based on our experience with young children, we became aware of the limitations of so-called 'standardized tests' with young children; many of which need to be administered and interpreted by someone with special training. The short attention span of many young children, their susceptibility to distraction and their generally poor motivation for taking tests at all are important drawbacks. Tests of general intelligence, which require qualified testers, may not present procedural difficulties, however, the global estimate of ability may not be of practical value to the teacher. Standardized tests give precise instructions for their administration, and while some allow the tester to repeat the questions, to encourage the child or to prompt, others do not. Changing the procedure has been shown to affect young children differentially. Some of the shorter, simpler tests of vocabulary, versions of which are still in use, we found to be unreliable with young children, for example that known as the EPVT (English Picture Vocabulary Test) or the similar PPVT (Peabody Picture Vocabulary Test). We found wide variation in the results of some children on a repeat testing, scores varying both upwards and downwards.

Semi-structured situations

These may be useful in eliciting from a child behaviour that reveals competence above that which was normally observed. In Chapter 3 we referred to the use of such situations by Tough in her research (Tough 1977). We used such procedures for story telling by the children. The child was taken to a quiet room or area, accompanied by a friend, and encouraged to choose a book from which to retell a story to the friend. In that situation we frequently elicited complex language mirroring the written language of the book, both in vocabulary and grammatical structure, often using the direct speech so common in books for young children. One young child of under 4 years of age gave an almost verbatim rendering of Jack and the Beanstalk, interspersed with simpler colloquial speech in his comments to his friend.

Such situations can provide the teacher with valuable insights on children's language. However, they must be distinguished from the administration of standardized tests, where less-well-qualified or less-experienced testers, for example, often provide prompts where these are not permitted, thus invalidating the results.

Observations

Over recent years many observational schedules have been developed for use in preschool settings and in primary schools and currently form part of the Foundation Stage Profile introduced into early years settings in England (QCA/DfES 2003). Observations in preschool units formed part of the longitudinal EPPE research, which is to be discussed in Chapter 6. They may be used to monitor particular children's development or choices of activities. They are helpful in assessing the effect of organizational changes in the setting or special educational interventions. There are problems for the person doing the observations, in not becoming a participant while observing or of causing changes in the behaviour of the children by not playing the role expected of an adult. When observing in the nursery schools we focused on particular target children, noting where possible examples of their language, the longest time they spent on particular activities, their approach to the activities and interactions with adults and other children. Such 'cameos' were helpful to the staff and sometimes provided them with new insights. It is very difficult to remain a non-participant observer, and I would argue that any researcher who believes they have no effect on the situation is being naïve. Before the advent of the sophisticated radio microphones it was essential for the observer taking notes to be close enough to hear what the children were saying. Even with radio microphones, background notes are important to flesh out the context for the dialogue.

Rating schedules

When direct observation or testing is not possible there is a temptation to provide rating schedules, to be completed by the adults, as a means of summarizing impressions. They are often relatively quick and simple to complete, and appear to be an easy way of getting information about the children. During our research we tried out a number of such well-known rating scales and found that many had quite serious limitations. Particularly important is the specificity of the categories and clarity of the questions.

> When studying any rating schedule, or developing one yourself, it is important to discuss its interpretation with a colleague. For example, we asked nursery nurses to give their definitions of terms such as 'frequently', 'sometimes' and 'very infrequently' in terms of number of times per day, per week, etc. We found many discrepancies in the interpretations of these terms. We also explored hypothetical terms with the nursery nurses based on real possibilities, for example 'completes puzzles'. For this we asked how they would categorize a child who rarely attempts puzzles, but completes them when he occasionally does so. Not surprisingly such statements produced considerable disagreement as to classification.

Our general conclusions based on the rating schedules we studied were that both the reliability and the practical pay-off were too low to warrant the effort in completing them. It seems important that a schedule is specific enough in identifying the situations in which particular behaviours are shown. We noted that when we asked different members of staff to complete the schedule for specific children, agreement between the assessors was not high. It is of course possible that the children really do behave differently with different members of staff.

> I suggest you look at a variety of rating schedules. Consider how specific the questions are and note the range of answers offered, then discuss these with a colleague. A useful exercise would be for two of you to observe the same child over a period and complete a rating schedule, then compare the results.

Recordings of children's language

The accurate recording of children's language in the complex and constantly changing environment of a preschool unit presents many problems; written narrative cannot capture what is often a continuous flow of dialogue between the young children. In our earlier studies in Dunbartonshire we were dependent on observation and note-taking, as were many other researchers at that time. In later studies in the West Midlands we initially used observational schedules, developed by Brenda Robson, one of my research workers, and later we were able to make a study of selected target children, each wearing a radio microphone. In two articles, Robson reports the dialogue between adults and children she was were able to record (Robson 1983a; 1983b). Details of the observation schedule, the language recorded and the implications for early education are to be found in Robson (1989). With the use of radio microphones on target children it was possible to record the speech of these children very clearly, and that of others within about 3 metres of the wearer.

> If you record the language of young children, you should note that it is likely to take you at least 8 hours just to transcribe a tape of 1-hour duration; that is before you attempt to analyse the material (Hart and Risley 1995). Hart and Risley also point out that although the recording of young children's language may be fascinating, its transcription and analysis is not only time-consuming, but also very boring.

Even if you are able to use a radio microphone you must appreciate the need for an observer to make context notes and the possibility that their presence may influence what takes place. See Chapter 3 for information on the techniques used by a number of researchers who recorded the language of young children in their homes.

Video recording

In our research in Dunbartonshire we were able to make a film showing selected episodes chosen by the head teachers illustrating their practice. This was valuable for stimulating discussion on the basis of the shared experience. At that time it was not possible to capture the naturally occurring events in the way that is now possible through the use of video. You might find some valuable ideas for studying preschool settings in the simple but effective technique used by Tobin for his research in preschool in three cultures: China, Japan and the United States. I wish this had been possible when we undertook our studies. He prepared a short edited video in one preschool in each country, ensured that it was acceptable to the practitioners as reflecting their practice, then used it as the basis for discussions comparing and contrasting their practice with others in that country and in the other two countries (Tobin *et al.* 1989).

Tobin has recently embarked on a more ambitious collaborative project in five countries, using the sophisticated technology now available for both recording and analysis of the data. The focus is on observations of the children and families of newly arrived generations in a preschool in England, France, Germany, Italy and the United States; the immigrant group chosen differs from country to country. The parents in the study will be newly arrived, live in one of the following cities and be of the following origins:

- Berlin, of Turkish origin
- Milan, and have been born in the Philippines
- Paris, of Algerian origin
- Phoenix, USA, of Mexican origin
- Birmingham, UK, Pushtu-speaking, with family members from Bangladesh and Pakistan.

These recordings will be edited to 20 minutes each; these videos will then form the basis for the discussions across and between the countries. Recently I was privileged to see some of the video material from the earlier study and pilot tapes for the new research. It will be some time before any results will be available. The study in England is directed by Professors Tony Bertram and Chris Pascal at the Centre for Research in Early Childhood (CREC) in Birmingham. The research is due to be completed in 2007.

> You could learn a great deal from preparing and editing even a very short video, and from discussions based on it. Remember to obtain permission from all those whom you plan to video, including the children, and the need to show the material to them first, clearing with them whether you can use it more widely. Be prepared to remove anything that any of the participants do not wish to remain. One interesting aspect of Tobin's first study, and our discussion in a seminar around the pilot tapes for the new study, is the fact that different people, for example from different cultures, do not necessarily show concern for the same incidents!

Chapter 6

Language and interaction in preschool units

Looking back and looking forward

INTRODUCTION

In this chapter I will discuss two of the major studies funded within the Nursery Research Programme in the 1970s, both frequently cited on reference lists (BERA 2003 for example). This is a modified version of Chapter 7 of *Children Under Five: educational research and evidence* (Clark 1988). One research within the programme was the major study funded by SSRC and directed by Jerome Bruner under the title Oxford Preschool Research Project, which ran from 1975 to 1978. Within that project there were a number of researches: observational and interactional studies in preschool units (nursery schools and classes and playgroups); studies in day nurseries; also studies of childminders and parents and preschool. The findings were reported in six books; the first by Bruner entitled *Under Five in Britain* (Bruner 1980) gives an overview and summary of the project. That and two of the other publications will be referred to in this chapter, namely *Childwatching at Playgroup and Nursery School* (Sylva, Roy and Painter 1980) and *Working with Under Fives* (Wood, McMahon and Cranstoun 1980). A number of later studies by Sylva and others have utilized the observation schedules developed within the project; these have also been used within playgroups and elsewhere for training staff in observational techniques. In a review of the project at the time of these publications I expressed concern at a number of aspects, including some of the statements made by Bruner in his overview which, after consulting the relevant research reports, I felt went beyond or were not borne out by the data.

The other research that I will discuss was directed by Corinne and John Hutt at Keele University, funded by the DES, and ran from 1975 to 1979. The report of the research submitted to DES in 1984 under the title *A Natural History of the Preschool* (Hutt et al. 1984) was a parallel study to that in the homes of young children reported here in Chapter 3. *Play, Exploration and Learning*, based on the research, did not appear until some years after the completion of the project (Hutt et al. 1989).

While these and the other studies funded within the programme were underway, there were already threats of cuts to preschool education, rather than the major expansion for which they had been planned. This had implications both for the willingness of preschool units to continue their co-operation in the projects and for the reaction of readers to any criticisms of preschool settings contained in the research reports. Only recently has there been a major longitudinal study in UK in which the effectiveness of preschool education has been evaluated and an assessment made as to whether some preschool centres are more effective than others in promoting the development of young children. The final report of this research, which was funded by DfES from 1997 to 2003, extended to 2004, appeared as I completed this book. At the end of this chapter I will give a brief outline of the EPPE research.

In Chapter 4 a framework was set out to help you when evaluating research. You should check these researches against that framework.

CHILDWATCHING AT PLAYGROUP AND NURSERY SCHOOL

This study and the following one, both part of the Oxford Preschool Research Project, were undertaken in Oxfordshire. While clearly it would have been unfortunate if all the studies in preschool education had been undertaken in areas of multiple deprivation, it is important to bear in mind where they did take place. Bruner cites reasons for the choice of Oxfordshire and the range of services included, stating that each service would be considered in terms of whether and to what extent it was fulfilling its function (rather than comparisons across types of provision); he stresses the limited budget and timescale (Bruner 1980: 53). It is important to note possible limitations in the selection of nursery schools, classes and playgroups as it is difficult not to become involved in comparisons across different types of provision.

Aim

The aim of this aspect of the research was to assess the extent to which the various contexts in preschool units stimulated complex activity, concentration and conversation between the children and between children and staff. This was studied by means of an observational schedule, with target children observed for 20 minutes on two occasions, with the activities recorded each half minute on an observation schedule. Speech was not recorded, thus only an approximate rendering could be included in the notes, and only when this was audible to the observer. None of the centres studied had special language tutorial schemes. A comparison was made, however, between units with more or less 'structure' in their day's routine.

The sample

The study took place in 6 of 14 nursery schools, 6 of 14 nursery classes and 7 of 120 playgroups. The sample is referred to as 'fairly representative' but no indication is given as to how this was assessed. Two quotations are important:

> We did not choose our centres randomly, as some were eager to collaborate in the study while others remained cool to outside research. . .
>
> our playgroups are probably drawn from amongst the better ones; that is most had well-established histories and highly trained staff.

> (Sylva *et al.* 1980: 46)

This would not be typical of playgroups at that time. Furthermore, reference is also made to seven organizers of the playgroups who had formal credentials in work with young children. Indeed in the composite pictures of the three types of unit, nursery school, nursery class and playgroup, the supervisor of the last is reported to be a trained primary school teacher who had given up practice when she started a family. The composite nursery school described had several teachers on staff as well as nursery nurses; the nursery class has one teacher plus other staff. Staff ratio is considered in relation to interactions.

> You should note that the term 'staff' is used for any adult regularly in the unit (including mothers in playgroups and students, but excluding visitors). This is important as reference is made to staff ratios when considering 'good' and 'very good' ratios.

Size of unit is another variable which is considered, however most of the large units were nursery schools and many of the playgroups were small.

The sample of children selected as targets for the observation were as follows: 120 children, with equal numbers in each of the three types of pre-school unit (nursery school, nursery class and playgroup); half of the children from each setting were aged 3–6 to 4–6 and half 4–6 to 5–6 years of age, which enabled comparison to be made between younger and older children. To quote (Sylva *et al.* 1980: 46), 'Although the centres studied were far from a random sample in the county, the individual children were selected on a random basis', from registers. Excluded were children with obvious physical handicaps or children who started school within the previous month. No reference is made to ethnic minority children, except in the composite picture of the nursery school where mention is made of a few such children attending (Sylva *et al.* 1980: 98).

Implications for early education

In considering the summary of findings in Bruner (1980), and the more detailed report (Sylva *et al.* 1980), the following points should be remembered: the definition of 'staff', the selective nature of the sample of units, and the area in which the study took place, namely Oxfordshire.

> You should be aware that you will not find information on the comparative role of teachers and other staff (including nursery nurses) in this study.

Size of unit is considered in relation to complexity of play and some important points are made on adverse effects of some large open-plan units. However, the nursery school singled out because of its positive dynamic pattern was indeed a large unit; thus size was not an inevitable barrier. Many new nursery schools built at the time of that research were large open-plan buildings, including those in Scotland in which I undertook the observational studies discussed in Chapter 5. The danger with large open-plan buildings, combined with free play for most of the day, is that far from resulting in complex play and dynamic interchanges they may lead to 'flitting' and distraction and low levels of activities. It may also be more difficult for staff to monitor the range of play of individual children. However, the authors stress that 'routine' and 'structure' may become a 'straitjacket'; this they demonstrate from a parallel study in Miami where the children spent most of the day in compulsory activities (see Sylva *et al.* 1980: ch. 9).

Units found to have what the researchers refer to as a higher 'task' structure were found to encourage greater complexity during the free play settings; even where most of the day was in freely chosen activity. The structure referred to is that of shared activities, not a formal language programme. On occasion children were found to choose to continue these activities when such a session was over; the activities also provided a common focus for children and staff for conversation. Bruner stresses that 'the findings surely suggest an interest and readiness in the children for more intellectually demanding tasks' (Bruner 1980: 71).

Limited evidence was found of conversations between adults and children; many of the interactions were of a one-off variety. Certain contexts were observed to stimulate more complex play, greater concentration and more extended dialogue. Much of the children's time was spent in interaction with their peers, and in this connection it was found that children in pairs were much more likely to engage in higher level play, suggesting that opportunities for such play should be encouraged. The activities found to be associated with more complex play were those with a clear goal and a means by which it could be determined when the goal had been achieved. Bruner refers to the importance of 'real-world feedback'. This meant that the children appeared to know at what they were aiming, whether building, drawing or doing puzzles.

With the younger children the pair setting seemed better; with older children play that also involved an adult was even more stimulating. It is commented that there was disappointingly little utilization of this in these units as a context for stimulation of complex play or extended dialogue.

> Even allowing for the limitations in this study noted above, there were important findings of relevance to preschool education, including the choice of activities, organization of the units and role of the adults. Its use of observational schedules also set the scene for later researches. Which of the findings do you think are still relevant? You will be able to check which of the findings were borne out in the more recent EPPE study, which also included observation and a wider variety of preschool units.

While it was possible to study turn-taking in conversation and the length of time an adult was engaged in conversation with a particular child or group of children, any evidence of the cognitive content of the conversation is based only on notes taken by the observer. One has to turn to other researches where the language was recorded during the free play settings for such information. Within one of the studies in the Oxford project there was evidence on language interaction between staff and children, based on recordings made and selected by staff in preschool units; this will now be considered.

CONVERSATIONS IN PRESCHOOL UNITS

In the introduction to *Working with Under Fives* Wood and his colleagues consider the priorities in aims of preschool practitioners as reported in other studies (Wood, McMahon and Cranstoun 1980). In any attempt to assess the extent to which such aims are reflected in practice you need to remember that a particular activity may serve a variety of purposes, and that time allocated to a particular activity is not a sufficient assessment of its priority. They stress the problems of translating aims into practice in preschool units, given the limited adult resources. They suggest it would not be practical for each child to be given sustained attention by an adult for long periods, they even question whether it would be advisable. They cite evidence from their own study and that of Sylva and her colleagues that adults faced with large groups of children and motivated to increase their personal involvement with them may push them into more directed group activities. To quote:

> Sylva's research suggests that such organised activities may well produce uninterested, passive children. Our own research, as we shall see, points in a similar direction... The practical question we must ask, given that practitioners accept the importance of their interactions with the child, is

whether they are able to translate their desires for interaction into effective practice.

(Wood et al. 1980: 11)

Aims and methods

Differences in style of language interaction between adults and children are explored by case studies based on recordings by practitioners (two nursery teachers and a playgroup supervisor). The question is raised as to whether differences in style matter, and whether this might be affected by the particular child's nature as well as the adult's. The incentive for this aspect of the study was concern expressed by a nursery teacher, in whose setting observations of interaction had taken place, that these did not capture the purpose behind what was observable (as noted earlier, there was no recording of the language). For this aspect of the research the language of selected interactions was recorded, using a small powerful microphone, then transcribed and analysed. The selection was the choice of the practitioner, who was able to add comments about the context and purpose behind the dialogue. The report presents three case studies and an analysis of the conversations. A further 21 practitioners were recruited to take part (19 playgroup workers and two teachers). The reasons given for a shift in emphasis to the playgroups is that for two of the researchers 'the principal contacts were in the playgroup movement', also 'that nursery schools are not very numerous around Oxford', and particularly:

> a growing concern about the cuts that were looming in the State sector, cuts that eventually culminated in the contraction of nursery provision in the county. The threat introduced by the economic and political climate was hardly conducive to a forward looking, research attitude.

(Wood et al. 1980: 32–3)

The above statement has been quoted because it shows a shift in emphasis within this study and explicitly states the change in climate even before these major studies had been completed, researches that had been planned to provide evidence for expansion of state-funded preschool education.

Findings and their implications

A statistical analysis of all the tapes of conversations indicated that the framework the adult offered for dialogue influenced the nature and extent of the children's responses. Frequent adult questions received answers, but little more, with the children less likely to elaborate on their answers, and were associated with fewer questions and contributions by the child. Topics of conversation were analysed and show how frequently the utterances by the adult were 'here and now' and how few were related to past or future. On hearing the tapes, a number of the practitioners who were recorded noted with regret that frequent attempts by children to engage in conversations about events elsewhere had failed because they had not understood them, or had not listened attentively enough. The frequency with which adults asked children questions to which they, the adults, already knew the answers is commented upon.

This study revealed the importance of practitioners becoming skilled in engaging young children in extended dialogue, and that it is not a simple task. A study of subsequent tapes of the three initial practitioners showed that they had been able to achieve a dramatic drop in management talk and to increase the length and, more important, the continuity of their con- versations. These three practitioners, all highly committed, are reported to have shown great flexibility. This was not true of all the adults involved in the study, as some, in attempting to be more involved in the children's play, increased their level of questioning or became more directive and controlling. Wood and his colleagues, based on their research, provide ideas for training of staff. Wood suggests in a later publication that one weakness of the Oxford study was that they did not have evidence about the children which would have enabled them to assess the extent to which some factors to do with particular children were responsible for some of the results. He therefore undertook a study with an experienced teacher, who was encouraged to change her style of conversation in ways that enabled the effect on specific children to be assessed. Wood and his colleagues later undertook extensive research with young deaf children in which they found similar evidence. Based on their research in preschool units with hearing children, and in special schools with hearing-impaired children, they provide a valuable structure for analysis of conversation, showing how different teacher strategies and levels of control affect the quantity and quality of the children's contribution (Wood *et al.* 1986: 53–64).

COMMENTS ON THE OXFORD STUDIES

The focus in the Oxford studies and the later research by Wood and his colleagues was on the role of the adult in the initiation and development of conversation rather than the possibilities in appropriate settings of peer–peer interaction, even with young preschool children. As will be shown in other studies, some of which I directed, peer–peer dialogue is not necessarily more limited, shorter or less cognitively demanding (see Chapter 8). It depends not only on the children, but also on the contexts that are provided within the unit. A study of such dialogue can also provide valuable insights for the adults, enabling them to improve their own practice and raise their expectations (see Robson 1983a; 1983b). As has been shown, their teaching style may facilitate or inhibit dialogue with and between the children. All the following are important:

- the plan of the setting
- the range of activities available
- the adults' perception of their role and their views of the children's competence.

PLAY EXPLORATION AND LEARNING

The context

The main studies in this section were funded by DES from 1975 and directed by Corinne and John Hutt. The final report to DES was entitled *A Natural History of the Preschool* (Hutt et al. 1984), later published as *Play, Exploration and Learning* (Hutt et al. 1989). Appendices in the book contain details of the observation schedules, etc., which you might find helpful if you are planning observational studies. In the parallel study discussed earlier, *The Young Child at Home* (Davie et al. 1984), a chapter is devoted to a comparison of the findings of the two studies. There are problems in making valid comparisons as the observations in the four types of preschool unit – nursery school and nursery class, playgroup and day nursery – were made during free play, while the children's activities were sampled at home over an entire waking day; different children were also involved in the two researches.

The main project in preschool units was undertaken in two contrasting areas; one area, the northern part of Staffordshire in the West Midlands, had a comparatively long tradition of support for nursery education, and included the area where the parallel study in homes was conducted. The provision of preschool education there was influenced by the demand for female labour and a local authority with interest in education of the young child. There were also day nurseries and many playgroups. The nursery tradition in the second area, parts of Cheshire, was very different; it was more recent and tended to be in nursery units or classes attached to schools. In the former, attendance was more likely to be full-time, in the latter part-time. Background information about units was obtained by means of a structured interview.

In the first area, all 21 nursery schools and six day nurseries were visited and a random selection was made of about one-quarter of the nursery classes and playgroups (11 of each). In one district studied, nursery classes were staffed by nursery nurses only, the head teacher of the school being in charge. All children in the day nurseries had extended day care, two-thirds of the children in the nursery schools and classes attended full-time, while no children in the playgroups attended full-time. The day nurseries had, as might be expected, the most children who suffered from difficulties and most mothers worked. About half of the mothers of the children in the nursery schools and classes worked, in the playgroups about 18 per cent worked, some worked only part-time or evening shifts. In the second area, the sample included seven nursery classes and one nursery school, and few children attended full-time. While about half the units reported that many mothers worked, this was mostly part-time.

> It is important to note that the children's home backgrounds differed in the various types of unit. This was also found in the recent EPPE study (Sylva *et al*. 2004a; 2004b).

The report presents the findings of a series of studies addressing different aspects of preschool education and using different samples; this makes it difficult to summarize the research while including information on the precise sample used for each aspect. You must bear this in mind when considering the findings, and if possible refer to the appropriate chapters in Hutt *et al.* (1989) to check for details. In Clark (1988) Chapter 7 I provided this detail when evaluating the research, based on their report to DES. In this chapter I will merely draw attention to the more important of their findings, with some indication of the samples. The following are the main aspects considered in the research:

- the activities and materials in the units and the use to which they were put by the children
- the aims of the staff
- adult activities and their influence on the children
- the children's span of attention and their choices
- types of play, with particular attention paid to fantasy play
- uses of language.

Activities and materials

The availability and use of materials and activities was observed in nursery schools, nursery classes, playgroups and day nurseries. Each unit was observed on two separate mornings at intervals of 20 minutes using a scan method of sampling. Immediately preceding the scan the observer recorded the various activities available; during the scan the number of children at the various activities was recorded. Free play periods were contrasted with periods of adult-organized activity where the children were constrained to attend. Comparatively little of the latter type of activity was observed in any of the four types of unit. Story and singing sessions occurred in all types of provision, while use of audio-visual aids was observed in nursery classes but seldom elsewhere. There were differences in the extent to which different types of activities were simultaneously available. The researchers report that there appeared to be some agreement among staff in the different types of unit as to the range of activities that were appropriate for children aged 3 to 5 years and also a belief in the value of play in the children's development.

The aims of the staff

The aims of the staff were explored using a brief questionnaire and information was obtained on the biographical details of the respondents. Staff in nursery schools and classes emphasized language development most. Staff in day nurseries stressed emotional security. Staff in playgroups stressed social-emotional development. A difference in perceived role was found between nursery nurses working in education settings and those in day nurseries. Many of the staff in the day nurseries were under 21 years of age; this was in contrast to staff in other types of unit, many of whom had children of their own. Greater emphasis was given by the staff in the nursery schools and classes to the role of the adult in giving guidance.

> At that time staff gave low ranking to the involvement of parents in the process of tuition, and the parents who were interviewed saw preschool as a means of preparing the child for the routine and discipline of schooling, rather than as an intellectual training. How much do you think this has changed?

Adults' activities

An observational study undertaken in a sample of each type of provision involved 11 staff from each type of unit. They were observed for 30 minutes on two separate days by means of time-sampling, with a check being made on inter-rater reliability. Staff spent comparatively short periods of time engaged in one activity before switching to another. Furthermore, involvement of adults in children's activities was found not only to be limited, but also to be brief when it did occur, partly, the researchers suggest, because of the free play situation.

When a check was made on which activities the staff regarded as most important it was found that a high value was placed on books, particularly by teachers. Playgroup supervisors were inclined to emphasize the value of water play and large climbing apparatus. Parents tended to emphasize academic activities. In the scans of the room it was observed that representational toys and the home corner were often used, in spite of the low value placed on those by the staff.

Children's activities

In order to study in more depth the involvement of the children in the various activities, 96 children (12 boys and 12 girls from each of the four types of provision) were selected and observed for two separate periods of 30 minutes. The effect on the children of the presence of an observer was assessed, and it appeared that this did not have a systematic effect on the children's play. Wide individual differences were found between children, but only in physical play were there significant differences, with more of this in the playgroups and with more boys than girls involved with such play. In spite of the stress placed by the adults on the importance of books, the children spent little time looking at books; a major influence on this could have been the importance of the presence of an adult for children to be stimulated to engage in this activity. This is in contrast to the findings of the research in a nursery school, which I reported in Chapter 5.

Most of the observations were indoors, but a small study was made in several nursery schools of 18 children aged from 3.5 to 4.5 years. Sex differences were found in the use of outside play areas.

Having established the range of materials available in the various types of provision, the researchers then turned their attention to what the children appeared to do with the various materials.

Use of materials

This aspect of the study involved 71 children in nursery schools and 59 from day nurseries. An interesting difference was found in the nature of play with dry and wet sand; the former was commonly associated with stereotyped repetition of two actions (though with younger children there were more exploratory patterns), but the latter showed much more varied sequences of behaviour. Water tended to be associated with an even greater range of patterns; it was observed that as the session progressed there was a need for adults to remove unwanted objects from the water.

'Product-orientated' activities, such as brush painting and clay and dough, produced different patterns of activities with the younger children, who engaged in more exploratory activities. Finger painting elicited a great deal of exploration, perhaps because of its novelty (it was rarely available). The social content of the activities, and whether there was an adult present, provided interestingly different patterns. For example, collage, where an adult was normally present, provided the child with a captive partner and some of the most sustained and lively discussions took place there. There was, however, most conversation with other children during sand and water play.

Fantasy play

There is a belief among many educationists concerned with young children that fantasy or imaginative play has an important role in children's cognitive development. This aspect of play was explored with a sample of nursery and reception class teachers of young children. Although all teachers were able to give examples of their own definition of imaginative play, there was no consensus as to its essential attributes. The researchers followed this enquiry with observation of fantasy play in nursery schools, studying groups of children at play. The aim was to make a study of the type of themes and their frequency, and of where in the classroom they were found. Most observations were indoors and they covered ten sessions of free play. The observer scanned the whole classroom, making detailed noted of incidents of fantasy play. These records were divided into 'episodes' and events within these.

Domestic themes were found to predominate (but with a sex difference). The availability of representational objects in a particular area was associated with a great deal of parallel play and relatively low level activity. Adults were seldom found to be involved in the fantasy play. Immaterial fantasy play might take place in various places, but was only apparent in about one-fifth of the events observed, usually involving groups of children, again seldom with an adult involved. A media theme was often involved in this type of play.

> There are interesting findings on fantasy play, but you should remember the limitations of this aspect of the research. The children's language was not recorded and knowledge of the verbal content of the play would be important in any assessment of its quality.

The general observations were followed by observation of 12 children aged about 4 years of age in a nursery school, 6 of whom were reported to show high levels of imaginative play and six low levels. These children's play was observed for 100 minutes during 20 observation periods. The children's language had been assessed on a standardized test and it was found that the amount and complexity of their fantasy play was closely related to the verbal competence they showed on the test.

As limited language of children in day nurseries had been observed in everyday utterances, the researchers decided to make a comparison of their language in fantasy play to check if in that context it was equally limited. In this instance a radio microphone was used and a detailed analysis was made of 12 children from each of 5 day nurseries. The children were found to show greater competence in their language in fantasy play than in their 'ordinary' speech with the young carers. Extensive extracts are provided of the children's language and these reveal that the expectations of children's language of the young staff were low, and they often adopted a manner that did not extend or expect any extended language from the children. However, it should be remembered that the researchers had found that developing language had not been ranked high by the staff in these units.

> You should remember that the fact that the more complex play and extended fantasy play were differentially seen among children who were linguistically

able does not enable us to assume a causal relationship, namely that complex fantasy play *per se* improves children's cognitive development.

The researchers stress that much of what they observed as fantasy play was repetitive, low level, not necessarily social and seldom involved adults. It is possible that there is a place for repetitive, low level, not necessarily social play, which may have an important recuperative function. One aspect not explored in this research was whether the children showing the most complex fantasy play and who were linguistically able came to the unit with these skills well-developed, and whether the home was reinforcing such activities. From the evidence of this research it seems that the presence of linguistically able children might be utilized to encourage more complex play in other children. The involvement of adults in the play could also raise the level of the play.

This aspect of the research raises many questions about the quality of fantasy play in preschool units at that time; whether there was a need for more planned and focused play, together with more involvement by adults whose training made them better prepared to engage in real dialogue with young children. What qualities do you think adults would require to enable them to encourage and sustain fantasy play in young children? How important do you feel 'props' are, and what kind would you use? Check other researches on fantasy play.

Attention and choice

Activity span, and in particular the role of the adult in extending children's attention, was studied, partly based on data collected in each type of unit. It was found that activity spans of the children without an adult were highest in the nursery school and class, but with an adult this increased in all types of unit. This showed the important role of the adult in stimulating and sustaining children's attention on an activity. The average length of activity span tended to be about a quarter of an hour, often with frequent interruptions; in a few cases, attention spans of anything from a minute to over an hour were observed.

An attempt was made to assess what, if any, features led children to be attracted to certain activities. It was found that girls more frequently chose activities where an adult was present than did boys; most of these approaches were child initiated. Children's departures from an activity seldom appeared to be aimless. However, it was noted that in product-orientated activities (those whose value had been stressed by Bruner), in many instances children left before the product was completed, and that this tendency was more common in boys. The picture presented is of children purposefully engaged, often in activities of their own choice, but with frequent interruptions. The importance of planning the position of the adults, and changes in the position of specific adults, became clear from observations in this research and other researches at this time.

Use of language

This involved 80 children aged 4 years of age in units from each type of provision, with equal numbers of boys and girls. Each subject was regarded as a target child and observed unobtrusively for two separate periods of 10 minutes. A study of the interaction suggested that some adults are more sought out by children than others, but the adult's nominal role may not be the explanation. Children tended more readily to approach an adult already involved in an activity with children. The findings were in accord with those of others in indicating that there was disappointingly little evidence of extended conversations between adults and children. One must consider whether any features of the environment could have militated against sustained conversations, as the evidence was similar from the various types of units. One common feature was that all had free play for most of the day. Attempts to respond to overtures from children appeared to result in only short and relatively superficial exchanges, possibly because of the sheer quantity and range of the demands with which the adults were bombarded. Furthermore, some children were rarely involved.

Types of play

The authors use the term 'play' throughout for the activities in which the children were involved because it was the term in common use by the staff. However, they make an important distinction between what they call 'ludic' behaviour, which is self-amusement, poorly focused and mood dependent, and 'epistemic' behaviour, which is concerned with acquisition of knowledge and information and is more focused. They suggest that at that time the environments in preschools were structured to encourage ludic behaviour more than epistemic behaviour, with day nurseries most so. They stress that epistemic behaviour is important for learning and cognitive development and that this requires a sufficiently good adult : child ratio for work with individual children and small groups. These researches showed, as did many of the others referred to throughout the book, that not only does there have to be an adequate adult : child ratio, but the adults must be trained to appreciate how to engage in dialogue with young children and to be sensitive to the needs of the children with more limited language development.

IMPLICATIONS FOR EARLY EDUCATION

The researches by the Hutts provided evidence from a wider range of preschool provision and in urban areas, much of which supported the evidence from the project directed by Bruner in Oxfordshire. During the course of the Hutt researches the behaviour of around 1,000 children in about 50 preschool units, nursery schools, nursery classes, playgroups and day nurseries, located in urban areas around Stoke-on-Trent and South Cheshire, was studied. Ethnic minorities were under-represented and children whose mother tongue is not English were not discussed. In all types of provision a wide variety of activities was potentially available; at the time of the research all were organized for free play, to which the staff were committed.

A number of the findings of these two researches were surprising to practitioners at the time, and many had important implications for the planning of preschool settings, choice of activities, the training of the adults and their role. The evidence on sand and water play and on fantasy play was disappointing as the behaviour there was often found to be stereotyped and limited, and adults were seldom available at these activities; they were more likely to be at clay, collage and painting. More children were present at a task when an adult was present. Adult and child interaction patterns were similar to those found in other studies, with limited conversation and many adult comments in the form of questions; explanations were infrequent (though more common in teachers).

> Consider which adult styles, organizational patterns and activities are associated with more extended and elaborated activities, greater concentration and more extended dialogue between adults and children, and between children themselves.

These studies illustrated the potential dangers of large free play settings as the entire context within which preschool children in large groups are placed, and the value of observational studies of target children in providing insights into the learning experiences of individual young children It is all too easy to visit a provision for young children and to believe, because of its air of involvement and activity, that it is stimulating for all children who attend. Observation of target children is also a valuable tool for practitioners aiming to improve their practice.

Observation backed by recording of the language of the adults and children in preschool units would support and extend the evidence from this study. A number of researchers began not only to use observation schedules, but also to record the language. In the study by Tizard and Hughes discussed in Chapter 3, for example, not only were recordings made of the girls' language interactions with their mothers in their homes in the afternoons, but also in the nursery classes in the mornings. They also found disappointingly limited interactions between the adults and the children in these latter settings. However, they did not report on the interactions between the children with their peers, some of which could have been stimulated by preceding conversations with the adults. In the researches I undertook in Dunbartonshire in the early 1970s, described in the preceding chapter, we undertook extensive observations in large open-plan nursery schools and were able to compare the chosen activities of boys and girls in the free choice settings prevalent at the time. We also studied the development of choices of play over time (that is between the 3- and 4-year-olds).

The large-scale longitudinal research into Effective Provision of Preschool Education (EPPE) which I will discuss briefly had a large sample of children, a range of different types of preschool provision and a complex design, which made it possible to assess many aspects of preschool provision.

> From what you have read so far, make a note of what you would expect EPPE to have identified as characteristics of effective preschool settings.

RECENT RESEARCHES INTO EFFECTIVE PRESCHOOL SETTINGS

As I complete this book the final reports of a number of researches into effective preschool provision are due, including those on Early Excellence Centres (EECs), Sure Start and EPPE. An EEC research has been undertaken by the Centre for Research in Early Childhood (CREC) in Birmingham (Bertram *et al.* 2002; 2004).

Sure Start is a government initiative that does not provide only one specific service, rather it is an effort to change and add to existing services; an early intervention for children aged 0–4 years, their families and the communities in which they live. The cost effectiveness of Sure Start (in England) in meeting its goals is being investigated by a national team led by Professor Melhuish of Birkbeck College, University of London. The research will run from 2001 to 2006/7; it has recently undertaken the study 'Fathers in Sure Start', a neglected area of research (Lloyd *et al.* 2003). Sure Start initiatives are also taking place in Scotland, Wales and Northern Ireland; the responsibility for early education and childcare rests with the devolved administrations.

A series of technical reports and many articles on EPPE are already available (Sylva *et al.* 2004a; 2004b) and the final reports have now been published (Sylva *et al.* 2004a; 2004b). A 5-year extension of the EPPE study, the EPPE 3-11 ESRC Teaching and Learning Research Study (2003–2008) will explore the effectiveness of primary schools and the continuing effects of pre-school, including the identification of children who have 'succeeded beyond the odds' (Siraj-Blatchford *et al.* 2004). For the discussion here I have consulted two of the technical papers, Technical Paper 4 (Melhuish *et al.* 1999) and Technical Paper 8a (Sammons *et al.* 2002), and articles by Sammons *et al.* (2004), Siraj-Blatchford and Sylva (2004) and Siraj-Blatchford *et al.* (2004).

The EPPE project, the first large-scale longitudinal British study on the effects of different kinds of preschool provision, was funded by DfEE (later renamed DfES) from 1997 to 2004; further linked projects are still underway, a follow-up of the children in primary school and an analysis of children termed to be 'at risk'. There is a related project in Northern Ireland. The initial sample was of approximately 3000 children from 141 centres in England representing six types of provision (Melhuish *et al.* 1999). The sampling procedures for geographical location, types of centre and children were complex.

> You will find from Technical Paper 4 that the parent, family and child characteristics were different for children attending different types of preschool. It is a useful source of information about the activities in the homes of the young children in the preschool sample, based on parental interviews.

Although for the majority of children in the sample English was the child's first language, there were 47 different languages used by children in the study; this varied within different types of preschool as did ethnicity and socioeconomic status. Of the children in the sample, 23 per cent were from ethnic minorities and ethnicity varied significantly between preschool centres.

The children were assessed at entry to the preschool setting, and again on entry to primary school.

An additional group of 300 home children, that is those who did not attend preschool provision, or at least only very briefly, was added as they entered primary school. These were selected from 96 different primary schools, those entered by the children in the main sample.

> You should note that in this recent research, as in previous studies, pockets of home children were unevenly distributed across the country and the characteristics of this group were different from the main preschool sample in important ways.

The children from ethnic minority groups were more likely to:

- have English as an additional language
- be from very large families
- have mothers who were not working
- be receiving free school meals.

Reasons for parents keeping their children at home were explored. The reasons included lack of appropriate provision nearby, a few parents wanted to teach their children at home, some were housebound, and others felt their child was too young to attend a centre (see Sammons *et al.* 2004). In the same article Sammons makes an important point based on the comparisons of child characteristics; that:

> these results indicate that the choice of different assessments to measure children's attainment at primary school entry may have equity implications... While the present findings are based on the particular set of

assessments used in the EPPE research, the issue is likely to apply to reception baseline schemes in general.

(Sammons *et al.* 2004: 697–8).

It is argued that a focus on mainly language-based measures for school reception assessment may disadvantage children of particular ethnic/language backgrounds.

> The point made above has implications for many types of assessment to which young children are subjected (see Chapter 5). I am stressing the problems of conducting such a research, rather than the findings, to help you appreciate just how complex a design is required to make comparison of the effectiveness of different types of provision, even of attendance at preschool. There are few children who do not attend primary school; however, Rothermel has undertaken a comparison which includes children educated at home, not only at the preschool stage but also instead of reception class (Rothermel 2004). Remember to check for evidence on the progress of children who do not attend school.

Technical Paper 8a reveals a further important feature when making comparisons between the effectiveness of centres, namely the importance of considering child mobility. Before starting primary school, 23 per cent of the children had left their target preschool centre and moved to other provision; mobility varied significantly for different types of provision. Children who did move were, in this research, followed to their new centres (Sammons *et al.* 2002).

The EPPE findings suggest that preschool can play an important part 'in combating social exclusion by offering disadvantaged children, in particular, a better start to primary school'. However, the research also 'points to a separate and significant positive influence of the home learning environment' (Sammons *et al.* 2004: 705). These findings, it is claimed, have had a considerable impact on government policy,

> where it is now recognised that investment in good quality preschool provision provides an effective means of reducing social exclusion and of breaking cycles of disadvantage.

(Siraj-Blatchford and Sylva 2004: 714).

> Perhaps you might feel that if this is true it is a sufficient justification for the funding which has been allocated to research on preschool education. The evidence from this research makes it clear that it is not sufficient to argue for the effectiveness of any particular type of provision.

The design of this research made it possible to go further and look at the particular pedagogic models and practices in the most effective settings. An extension of the EPPE research made this possible. The Researching Effective Pedagogy in the Early Years (REPEY) research involved intensive case studies (see Siraj-Blatchford and Sylva (2004) for a brief outline of the research design); this included systematic target-child observations during 2 weeks of intensive case study in 14 settings. Briefly, the following are among the aspects considered:

- sustained shared thinking
- diversity and differentiation
- discipline
- indoor space
- home educational provision.

It seems appropriate to complete this chapter with quotations from the above article, which reinforce the findings of the researches reported in the earlier parts of this chapter and elsewhere in this book. The following extracts are all from the same page:

> The learning environment must, therefore, provide very young children with opportunities to be active and to take the initiative to learn. . .

> the teacher/adult having an awareness of, and responding to the child's understanding or capability vis-à-vis the particular subject/activity in question. . .

> the child's awareness of what is to be learnt. . .

> the active co-construction of an idea or skill.

> (Siraj-Blatchford and Sylva 2004: 727)

Both participants contribute to the learning process, although not necessarily in equal terms or to an equal extent. Siraj-Blatchford and Sylva argue that the provision of exploratory play environments, such as sand and water, therefore will only be effective 'if the materials/apparatus are chosen carefully to provide cognitive challenge'. They stress the importance that the outcomes are 'either modelled, demonstrated, explained or otherwise identified in the children's experiences and actions, and encouraged' (Siraj-Blatchford and Sylva 2004: 727). They do allow a place for opportunities for the children to have free play and exploration.

It was found that children tend to make better intellectual progress in fully integrated centres, which combine care and education, and in nursery schools, and in settings with staff that have higher qualifications, especially with a high proportion of trained teachers on the staff (Siraj-Blatchford *et al.* 2004).

In the near future you will be able to consult not only the final report of the EPPE and related REPEY studies, but also many articles reporting aspects of the research that I have not mentioned here. I suggest you reread the earlier part of this chapter. You will find that the foundations for an analysis of what makes an effective preschool setting were beginning to be identified in the researches in the 1970s and 1980s. Remember that the children in the EPPE study were 3 years of age in 1997. Consider how the relevance of the findings will be affected by the fact that preschool education in Britain is now available for all children aged 4 years, and for those aged 3 years whose parents wish it for them.

Section III

Continuity, communication and learning in early education

Chapter 7

Research studies on transition and continuity in early education

Lessons from the past

BACKGROUND

Most children in Britain will now have had experience in at least one preschool unit before entry to primary school. Currently some children may be experiencing two different preschool settings consecutively, or even in parallel. There are many points of transition in early education where conflict in expectations can occur: between home and school, between different stages within the same setting, as well as from one type of provision to another.

> Before you read this section consider what types of transition may cause problems for young children and their parents and what types of conflicts in expectations might arise. You can then compare your list with those identified in the researches I will discuss. You will find that transition is a topic of current interest in early education in many countries.

'Continuity' in the education of young children was one of the priority areas for research identified by the Department of Education and Science (DES) in 1975. It was recommended that there should be studies of children's experiences in school between the ages of 3 and 7 or 8 years of age. It was hoped that there might also be a development project to 'illustrate ways of achieving continuity and progress of experiences for children in the age range' (DES 1975b: 72). Unfortunately the researches that were funded tended to consider transition rather than continuity, and to focus on a very short timescale and on mainly organizational aspects rather than curricular progression. The urgency expressed (to obtain evidence to influence policy), together with limitations in funding, may partly explain the nature of the studies. Nevertheless many of the issues concerning transition and continuity identified in the studies the 1970s and 1980s are still pertinent. In this chapter brief reference will be made to a number of the studies. The following researches will be considered:

- two researches undertaken by the National Foundation for Educational Research: one on transition from home to preschool, the other from preschool to primary
- a study funded by a teachers' union on transition into reception class
- an investigation funded by the Scottish Education Department (SED) into the role of the parents during children's transition into primary school
- a longitudinal study in which the educational experiences and attainment of boys and girls from indigenous white and Afro-Caribbean backgrounds are compared
- a study of 4-year-olds in reception class.

All but the last two are considered in detail and evaluated in Chapter 13 of *Children Under Five* (Clark 1988), and the other two are discussed in Clark (1989). Here I will give a brief outline of the studies and indicate issues identified by the researchers. In chapters 8 and 9 I will consider in more detail a study I undertook in the West Midlands on young children from different ethnic backgrounds who were observed in a variety of settings preschool and in their first year in primary school.

At the time of these researches, the 1980s, of course only a limited number of children did have experience in a preschool unit, and there were wide differences in provision from one area to another.

> You should remember that although currently in Britain there is preschool provision for most 4- and 3-year-olds, attendance still remains voluntary. Thus for some children entry to primary school might be their first experience beyond their home environment, as it was for many at the time of these researches.

If you are working in England, one key transition now could be at the end of the Foundation Stage, on transfer from reception class to Year 1 in the primary school, at about 5 years of age (QCA/DfES 2003). In Scotland the curriculum for children between 3 and 5 years of age meshes with the curricular guidelines for primary school, and the above terms are not used. Primary 1 is the first year in primary school, not reception class (see SCCC 1999, now Learning and Teaching Scotland).

THE FIRST TRANSITION: BLATCHFORD, BATTLE AND MAYS

This research concerned transition from home to preschool unit (Blatchford, Battle and Mays 1982). In the report entitled *The First Transition: home to preschool* the authors stress the importance of considering transition prior to entry and in terms of a continual interplay between experiences at home and school.

The sample

Seven local authorities were involved with questionnaires to nursery schools and classes and with interviews of staff. In four of the authorities playgroups were also sampled. However, in the latter the response rate to questionnaires was low: 68 per cent. The research also involved observational studies in two local authorities of 51 children during their first three 3 in nursery class. The parents of some of the children were also interviewed, but no observations took place in the homes.

Findings

Wide differences were found in policy with regard to parents remaining in the unit during the initial stages of the child's attendance and the extent of parental contact with staff. Staff questioned on children's initial reactions reported varied patterns, with some children flitting from one activity to another and others forming an attachment to a specific member of staff. The average age of children on entry was 41 months (the age range is not stated).

Reference is made to the different types of behaviour exhibited by the children on entry. The researchers refer to one group of children as 'distressed'; generally poor in intellectual ability, in their attitude to teachers and pupils and in concentration. A second group they refer to as 'bright constructive'; busily involved in constructive gross activities. A third group was 'child relaters'; clearly interested in contacting other children. The researchers claim that a fourth group showed a preference for relating to adults, which influenced the activities they selected.

The children in this study were observed only for their first 3 weeks and during the ninth week in the preschool setting. It would require a more lengthy observational study to ascertain how long lasting are children's initial reactions to a strange environment and how this is influenced by the setting and approach adopted by the staff.

There was an attempt to relate these tendencies to pre-entry experiences. This must, however, be treated with extreme caution and certainly no causal relationship could be established as the children were *not* observed in their home setting prior to entry, information was from parental interviews.

The mothers of 30 of the children were interviewed after their children had attended for a term. Although parents were reported to be 'satisfied', this was based on little informed knowledge, most was gained from their children. They also seemed confused as to what part they could play in helping their children. The authors suggest that the parents tended to undervalue their own influence and not to appreciate that many everyday activities they did with their children, such as reading stories and looking at books, were of significance towards learning to read.

> It would be interesting for you to consider the extent to which the many projects for parents and preschool children, including with babies, over the intervening years have increased parents' awareness of the value of their contribution to their children's early learning.

AND SO TO SCHOOL: CLEAVE, JOWETT AND BATE

This study was undertaken between 1977 and 1980, and was published in the book entitled *And So To School: a study of continuity from preschool to infant school* (Cleave *et al.* 1982). The timescale of the research was relatively short, thus transition rather than continuity was the focus.

The sample

The children, who were in four different local authorities and entered 12 different infant schools, were selected randomly from the transfer lists. The 36 children who were studied in detail were observed only during the last 6 weeks before entry to infant school at the preschool unit or home, and for the first 6 weeks at infant school. Their subsequent experiences and progress were not monitored. A further limitation is that there was only one child who entered infant school direct from home. She was rather atypical of such children, as her mother, even with knowledge of preschool provision, had made a choice to keep her at home.

> However, you should note that the researchers only included children who had a good record of attendance and consider in what ways that might have influenced the results.

Findings

One aspect of this study involved constructing a joint profile for preschool units and another for infant classes from 'pooled' information from large numbers of preschool units and infant classes. A comparison of these revealed striking differences between the two settings in the main types of activity available to the children and in organization. Profiles drawn even from large samples, as in the above research, may mask a great deal of variation *within each type of unit*. In addition, what transition may mean for particular children, and their parents, does not 'come alive' from such an analysis. Therefore, these researchers also observed target children in preschool units prior to transition, then in the reception class after transition.

The observations revealed how different might be the adult expectation with which the children had to cope before and after transition. The following important differences are noted:

- While in the preschool unit, *play* was likely to be the medium through which learning was expected to take place, *work* became important after transition, with play relegated to playtime or a reward for work well done (or at least completed).
- Children who had been *free to move around* in the preschool unit found *less mobility* was permitted.
- *Talk with peers*, which had been positively encouraged, was *no longer acceptable*.
- *The length of time* devoted to particular activities was *more constrained*, and determined now by the adults rather than, as previously, mainly by the children.
- In a number of ways the *children became more dependent* on the adult, not more independent.

Our findings in the study of early education and children from ethnic minorities were similar, see chapters 8 and 9.

STARTING SCHOOL: BARRETT

During 1985/6, a study of transition was commissioned by one of the teachers' unions, the Assistant Masters and Mistresses Association, whose members were concerned about the behaviour of children on starting school, and whether this had deteriorated in recent years. As one aspect of her study of *Starting School*, Barrett observed selected children before and after transfer, at home and at school (Barrett 1986).

The study

This was a brief study, only September 1985 to June 1986, and had two phases. The first phase was collaborative with teachers, who observed their own reception classrooms, activities and organization, and target children's responses at the beginning of each term. Details of the background of the schools were also collected. The second phase (like that of Cleave *et al.* 1982) involved observation of children in a playgroup or nursery during the month prior to their entry to school and for their first month in the primary school. Parents were also involved in making observations of their children at home, and were interviewed. Following the case study, the factors which appeared to influence the children's responses were discussed with the wider group of teachers involved in the other aspect of the project.

The findings

In addition to providing information for others, the involvement by the teachers heightened the awareness of those who participated of the wide individual differences in the children's needs and responses. Like others, Barrett found differences between what was on offer to young children in preschool units, on entry to reception class and at home (Barrett 1986). This is of course not surprising; what is disturbing, however, is her evidence that for some of the target children the preschool unit provided not only a wider curriculum but also one which was more challenging than that in reception class. Likewise some children showed impressive skills at home which they were not expected or encouraged to demonstrate in the classroom; indeed, she found that the special interests and knowledge that the children developed at home were barely evident at school. Barrett found that:

- children had to learn 'survival' skills and to cope with 'not knowing' and the feelings this might arouse
- the children in the reception class, now somewhat older, had to rely on the teacher indicating exactly what to do, and whether what they had done was correct, and not only as regards the bounds of permitted behaviour
- for some children there was an increase in inactivity, in time when they were uninvolved, were waiting for the attention of the teacher or seemed uncertain what they should do
- the class soon came to appear *more homogenous*.

The aim of the case study was to raise issues for further exploration; practical implications are also discussed (see Barrett 1986: 130 onwards). Bear in mind that this case study was undertaken using only one class, that the children were relatively comparable in age and were 'rising fives' on entry to reception class. For most of these children reception class was not their first experience of a group setting, indeed most entered school with companions from the same playgroup only minutes away from the school.

Consider how different might be the experiences of other children on starting school. Were you to undertake a study such as this you might find some helpful ideas in Barrett's report. For example, she used photographs of young children in a variety of reception classroom settings to encourage young children to express their views. Most revealing were the children's interpretations of contexts, which they related to their own.

CONTINUITY IN EARLY EDUCATION – THE ROLE OF THE PARENTS: WATT AND FLETT

A research project, commissioned by the SED, was carried out in Scotland during 1983/4 by Watt and Flett (1985). They adopted a 'case study' approach to investigate in some depth continuity and the role of the parents in three primary schools and in related preschool provision. Each primary school was in a different region of Scotland, selected to provide as much variety as possible in types of preschool provision and other relevant aspects. As the researchers had limited funding and a short timescale, they selected schools which, while giving variety, were relatively accessible to Aberdeen, which was their base (within a 160-kilometre area).

You should bear in mind that the place of work of educational researchers is likely to have influenced the geographical area in which their research is conducted; this is particularly true in more detailed intensive studies requiring frequent visits to schools or homes. When you read research reports remember to consider what might have been the effect on the results had an investigation been undertaken: in a different area (say rural rather than urban); with more or fewer children from ethnic minorities (or from different minority groups); or with more or less adequate (or different) preschool provision.

The report not only gives an idea of the sources from which their evidence was collected and the way the researchers themselves acted as participants during the relatively brief study, it also contains a survey of literature available at that time on continuity and the role of the parents. They identified three general points:

- Parents are in the best position to provide long-term continuity for their children, and the issue is how best to achieve this.
- Schools and preschool groups are normally concerned to ease transition between one stage and the next and tend to see this within the framework of their own professional assumptions.
- Problems appear to arise when attempts are made to link these types of continuity because the level and type of parental involvement, either expected or acceptable, varies so much from setting to setting.

Understanding the nature of transition from preschool to reception class, or from one stage in the primary school to another, as it is faced by individual children is greatly helped by observational studies of selected children. Likewise, the case-study approach adopted by Watt and Flett, with its focus on specific primary schools and the related preschool settings, is a valuable way of capturing the issues faced by individual schools. Survey-type studies and researches using questionnaires on attitudes of parents and professionals inevitably miss the subtleties of the issues. From these it is difficult, probably impossible, to identify personalities and practices in sufficient detail for their roles in promoting or preventing continuity for the child, and contact with the parent, to be assessed. We should not underestimate the power of just one individual in a key position to facilitate or prevent communication.

In their report Watt and Flett (1985) consider the implications of the study for early education, and Watt has developed these points further in an article in which she stresses the need for 'compatibility' without 'sameness', and 'stimulation' without 'shock' in the early learning experiences of young children (Watt 1987). She indicates the following major difficulties in providing 'continuity with extension' in early education:

- inadequate provision of preschool education
- parents, and even some primary school teachers, may see preschool education only in terms of preparation for school
- the short period that children spend in preschool education and the fact that children may move in and out of several types of provision
- the danger that pressures for co-ordination of preschool services may lead to a neglect of links between preschool and primary.

Some problems may indeed have been exacerbated following the introduction of the National Curriculum in England and Wales, which resulted in the exclusion, at least for a period of years, from many educational debates of practitioners concerned with children under 5 years of age; that is, below statutory school age. An attempt has been made recently in England to correct this by the introduction of the Foundation Stage to bridge the transition from preschool to reception class, the first year in primary school (QCA/DfES 2003).

Consider which of these points are still relevant and could stimulate ideas for further research.

YOUNG CHILDREN AT SCHOOL IN THE INNER CITY: TIZARD ET AL.

A longitudinal study run from 1982 to 1985 compared the educational experiences and attainment of boys and girls from indigenous white and Afro-Caribbean backgrounds in a number of primary schools in the Inner London Education Authority from the time of their entry to reception class through their infant schooling to about 7 years of age (Tizard *et al.* 1988). The aims of the study were to 'throw some light on the factors in the home and the school that affect attainment and progress in the infant school, and in particular the factors that might account for differences in the school attainment of boys and girls and black and white children' (Tizard *et al.* 1988: 167).

The researchers felt that:

- a longitudinal approach was essential, whereby the same children were studied over a period of years
- the children should be assessed prior to their entry to primary school to check whether there were differences in pre-entry skills between the groups
- the children's attainment and their relative progress should both be assessed over the period of study
- the school and home influences on progress during the first years in the infant department should both be assessed
- social disadvantage between the two ethnic groups could best be controlled by selecting children of Afro-Caribbean ethnic origin and the indigenous white children from the same schools
- their sample should be so constituted that they could make comparisons between boys and girls, within the two ethnic groups, and in terms of progress
- they should interview the children to get their views on their academic success, and other aspects of their infant school experience, something not included by some other researchers.

You should begin to see the inevitable complexity of the research design needed for all these aspects to be investigated.

This is an important study for a number of reasons.

- It is longitudinal, and thus it is possible to relate children's attainment to their level of knowledge before entry to primary school, and their final achievement to their progress at different stages.
- It includes both information on the views of the teachers about the curriculum and observation in the classrooms each year of what actually took place.
- By observation of selected children it was also possible to see to what extent the curriculum offered differed for individual children depending on the school they attended, even the classes in which they were taught, and/or their level of attainment on entry to each class.
- The nature of the sample makes it possible to compare the attainment of boys and girls at each successive stage, and, within each sex, the attainment of indigenous white children and children from Afro-Caribbean

backgrounds. For that reason it was necessary to assess pre-entry skills and to observe the children throughout their early years in school to identify whether and when differences in attitude and attainment took place.

- At the initial stage differences were not found between children from the two ethnic backgrounds in this sample where the school attended was matched, the children came from the same nursery class, and the social backgrounds were comparable. This was important information to have against which to consider any later differences which might be found.

The sample

In order to have access to a sample with known characteristics immediately prior to entry to reception class the researchers selected their sample by testing the children about to transfer to primary school who were attending the nursery class in 33 primary schools in which they hoped subsequently to undertake the observation and assessment on achievement. Thus, all children in the study had attended nursery class, which as the researchers point out was common for children in Inner London, where the study took place.

> It is important to note this constraint, and to consider whether the results might have been different, and in what ways, if it had involved children who had *not* attended nursery class. Remember that from this research you cannot assess the effects of attendance at nursery class on either the children's attainment or parental attitudes.

The focus in this study was relative performance of indigenous white children and Afro-Caribbean children, a choice made because of evidence of differences in attainment of these groups at later stages in the school (see Tizard *et al.* 1988: ch. 1 for a review of the literature on achievement in relation to social class, sex and ethnic background). Children of Asian ethnic origin are not included in this research.

One major difficulty in a longitudinal study, particularly one of this length, is how to minimize any loss from the sample and how to assess the effects of any loss which does occur.

> Consider all the aspects in this research where a loss of some of the sample was possible, and how important such losses might be. Armed with this information you may find it easier to follow the arguments in the research report, which is couched in rather technical language. The issues involved in any assessment of the relative influence of the whole range of school and home factors on children's progress and attainment in early education are highly complex.

The findings

The research by Tizard and her team is important as it is one of the last researches into the curriculum in the early years in Britain prior to the introduction of the National Curriculum in England and Wales and national assessment of all children at about 7 years of age. In view of the reasons given by the Government for these initiatives, claims that they are necessary to raise standards, it is worth studying Chapter 11 of their research and noting their comments:

- Parents had a big influence on the level of preschool attainments, but factors within the school were more important once the children started school.
- The two major factors associated with progress in the infant school were the range of 3R curriculum taught to the children and the expectations that the teachers had – the wider the curriculum, the better the children's progress.
- The children's progress depended to a large extent on the schools they attended, and more particularly the classes within which they were taught.
- There were wide differences between schools and classes in what children of the same age were taught, which could not be accounted for by the intake to the school.
- Teachers had expectations not only of individual children, but also of whole classes.

The great majority of children were being taught a narrow range of subjects in a fairly traditional way. Thus the researchers claim to dispel myths about British infant schooling, including that in the infant classrooms learning tends to be through 'discovery' or play. They found little discovery learning or working in groups. To quote: 'We also saw no case for arguing that a core curriculum is necessary for infant schools, or that they should go "back to the basics"' (see Tizard *et al.* 1988: 174–5).

The literacy and numeracy strategies may, at least in England and Wales, have placed greater constraints on the teaching in the early stages of the primary school. League tables, for 7- and 11-year-olds may well have added further constraints as the schools attempted to raise their average achievement. At least for some time, the curriculum in the early stages of primary school might have become even more limited than these researchers found in the 1980s.

A GOOD START?: BENNETT AND KELL

One further research whose findings are of relevance to the relationship of teacher aims and practices to the learning experiences of individual children in the classroom is that by Bennett and Kell (1989). The aim of the study was, by a focus on observation of 'target' children in classrooms, to identify the extent to which teachers' intentions are translated into specific activities whose purpose is made explicit to the individual child, and at an appropriate level, and whose success is appropriately monitored.

Make sure you appreciate what this implies before reading further! Some of these findings are not likely to be specific to reception classes.

The sample

The focus was on 4-year-olds in the infant school within a sample selected to give representation of as wide a range of policies for admission to reception class as possible. Neither the design nor the findings are likely to be reception-class specific; thus it would be interesting to use a similar design to compare the choice and explicitness of focus in learning activities which teachers provide for children in other classes in the primary school, or children of a similar age who happen still to be in preschool units.

The research, which had two linked stages, was conducted in three local authorities, which had different policies for children's admission to reception class: in one LEA, admissions were once a year, in the second termly, and in the third twice per year. As a consequence, a different age range was admitted in each local authority. For the initial stage of the research, 20 schools from each local authority were selected to represent different types and sizes of school and catchment areas. Head teachers and reception class teachers were interviewed to obtain factual information and, by using more open-ended questions, their aims and policies for 4-year-olds. Even in a sample of local authorities selected in this way there would be many other differences between schools in addition to the authorities' intake policies, making any comparison of the effects difficult. Some of these differences concerned whether children attended part day only (and if so for how long), the availability of auxiliary and parental help (and for how long), the age distribution in the class (which could be from a few months to several years), the resources, size of class and classroom, and not least the qualifications and experiences of particular reception class teachers.

For the classroom observation, two children per class were observed for a minimum of three half days in the spring term, with approximately 16 hours of observation of activities per classroom. The report is based on observation of 22 children in 11 schools in two LEAs.

The findings

It was found, as in other studies, that the children in these reception classes tended to:

- work individually rather than collaboratively (even when seated in groups)

- be more often seated rather than active
- mainly undertake activities chosen by the teacher.

Limited evidence was found that any play activities in the classroom were successfully planned as an effective learning experience with explicit goals. The results are presented with examples from the activities observed which are analysed in terms of their appropriateness to the teacher's stated goal and the child's performance.

This research presents yet more evidence on just how different may be the educational experiences in the classroom of individual young children in Britain, even at a given point in time. One disturbing finding from the interviews was the difference in the reception class teachers' stated aims and their curriculum priorities, the former related to feelings (such as to enable the children to develop confidence and to be happy); the latter to more cognitive aspects. Other worrying findings from the observation study were: just how often when setting an activity the teacher failed to indicate, or indicated wrongly to the child its intended purpose; and the teachers' willingness to regard the activity as having been successful in outcome even though its aim had not been achieved, for example if the child had been busy.

> Thus, you need to consider not only the expressed aims of practitioners and their stated curriculum, but also the translation of both into the learning experiences provided for the individual young children in the classroom and the ways their success is monitored.

TRANSITION FROM PRESCHOOL TO PRIMARY

The researches discussed so far have raised a number of issues of relevance to children's transitions within early education, including the following:

- Organizational differences may be found within the classroom; some may be related partly to the presence in many classes in primary schools, even in the early years, for all or part of the day of only one adult, the class teacher. Recently the government has funded an increase in the number of teaching assistants in primary schools. However, assessments of the use of the teaching assistants suggest that their duties and allocation across classes vary greatly from one school to another (see Clark 2002).
- The reception class, or other class in the primary school, is part of a much larger unit to whose demands it must be tailored, and some of whose facilities it must share.
- The extent to which what the child does during the day is a matter of choice on the child's part may vary; surprisingly, perhaps, less choice is available to the older child in the infant department. This may be

influenced by differences in teacher views on curricular content or demands from central government.

- The relative educational value placed on play may differ greatly. Play may change from the valued way of presenting the curriculum and be relegated to an activity confined to the playground or a reward for work completed.
- There may be dramatic differences in the numbers of children with whom a child must make contact after entry to primary school. Coupled with this, however, there may be little opportunity for sharing of educational experiences in the classroom.
- The parents (or more usually the mother) may be expected to adopt a very different role when the child is preschool age from that expected once the child enters the primary school. You would note that many parents underestimated their contribution to their child's education.

Thus, there may indeed be discontinuity, or even conflict, between the aims set for children and the teachers' expectations for parental contribution within different stages of early education. Furthermore, as I mentioned earlier, even with preschool education available to all 3- and 4-year-olds, there will still be some children who enter primary school direct from home. It would be interesting to know whether similar studies in other classrooms, with children with a wider variety of prior experiences or a different or wider age range on entry, would give comparable results.

A telephone investigation has been conducted to investigate the challenges faced by head teachers and reception class teachers in implementation of the new Foundation Stage for ages 3–5 years (Aubrey 2004). *A Study of Transition From the Foundation Stage to Key Stage 1*, which covers primary schools in England and is funded by the DfES, has been undertaken by the National Foundation for Educational Research (NFER) (Sanders *et al.* 2005). The aim is to provide evidence on how best to support children's learning during transition. It is thought there may be important differences across schools and sub-groups of children in managing successful transition. It is possible that weaker schools and children from disadvantaged backgrounds may find the inherent discontinuities particularly difficult.

In the following two chapters evidence will be presented from the study I undertook in five primary schools in the West Midlands with different proportions of children from ethnic minorities.

Chapter 8

Communication in the early education of children from different ethnic backgrounds

Part I of a DES-funded study

BACKGROUND

The findings of our research discussed in this and the following chapter are still of relevance today. Indeed had I not indicated that it took place between 1982 and 1984 you might well have believed it to be a contemporary study. None of the researches summarized in the previous chapter considered the problems of children whose mother tongue and first language was not that used in the school, whose parents' expectations might be different from those of the teachers, with whom they might have difficulty communicating. Yet, as we found in our research on children with special needs in preschool units in the West Midlands in 1981/2, even by that time, in some schools the majority of the children were from minority ethnic groups, though the proportion varied widely from school to school. In the 1980s in Birmingham, already about 25 per cent of the births were to parents of Asian ethnic background; a further 9 per cent had at least one parent of Afro-Caribbean ethnic origin.

> Consider just how many cultures and languages are now represented, in many inner city schools in particular, and what problems these present for the children and parents as well as the staff. (See Clark 2003 and 2004 for articles on the implications of the census for education in England and Wales and in Scotland.)

We received funding from DES in 1982/3 for a one-year project in five primary schools in the West Midlands, with limited additional funding in 1983/4 for interviews of the reception class teachers and the parents of some of the children from ethnic minority backgrounds, and also so that the children whose mother tongue was Punjabi could be retested in English after a year in primary school. The research had two full-time researchers, Jennifer Barr and Wendy Dewhirst; related projects were undertaken by several of my master's degree students. The research report was submitted to DES in 1984 (Clark, Barr and Dewhirst) and subsequently a number of papers were published by the team and by several of my students. We had gained some experience in the use of radio microphones in the research I had undertaken on children with special needs, which had enabled us to record the language of young children in a variety of free play settings (see Robson 1983a; 1983b; 1989). Such equipment was still in its early stages of development (see Tizard and Hughes 1984, who used radio microphones in their study of young girls in their homes and in preschool, discussed in Chapter 3).

Unfortunately it may no longer be possible for readers to obtain the full report of this research as submitted to DES. For that reason I have cited mainly papers by members of the team and some of my former students who took part in the research. This will provide information on some aspects of the study; it will also indicate how ongoing research can act as a stimulus for student projects. In this chapter I have decided to bring the research alive by providing details not only of the planning of the research, but also by including samples of the language of the children which we recorded in a variety of settings. In Chapter 9 I will discuss our observations on the different reception classroom settings as contexts for learning, the views of the teachers about early education, and the views of the parents whom we interviewed. Reference will also be made to the schedules developed during the second year of the study for interviews of the reception class teachers and the parents of some of the children from ethnic minorities.

AIMS OF THE RESEARCH

The research was planned to investigate in five primary schools the similarities and differences in classroom environments within which children from different ethnic backgrounds spent their first year in primary school. The aims of the research were:

- to assess the range of competence of the children and the extent to which this appeared to vary in different contexts and over time
- to identify features in school generally and in the classroom organization and practice that appeared to facilitate communication with and between these young children.

THE SAMPLE

Five primary schools were selected, three in Birmingham and two in Sandwell, chosen for their varied proportions of children from different ethnic backgrounds, for some of whom English was not their mother tongue. The policy for entry to reception class differed in the two authorities. At that time, in the three schools in Birmingham children entered in the term before their fifth birthday; in Sandwell children entered at the beginning of the year during which they would have their fifth birthday (a policy later adopted by Birmingham).

The two large schools, both in Sandwell, had their own nursery class attended part-time by most of the children prior to entry to reception class. One of the smaller schools also had its own nursery class. The two remaining smaller schools, which were in newer buildings, did not have a nursery class, but a number of their children attended one of the nearby nursery schools.

The children who were studied were the 247 who entered reception class during 1982/3; observation took place in seven of the nine classes with reception class children, and within these, selected children were investigated in more detail. Most children entered reception class having attended some form of preschool unit (77 per cent), though few attended playgroup or day nursery. We had observed some of the children and recorded their language in the preschool unit before the funded research commenced. Indeed the availability of this information influenced the choice of primary schools.

The ethnic origin of the children studied was as follows:

- indigenous white: 102
- at least one parent of Asian ethnic origin: 83
- at least one parent of Afro-Caribbean origin: 59
- other: 3.

The mother tongue of most of the children with an Asian ethnic origin was the same, namely Punjabi.

The intake to each of the two large schools was about 60 children, all entering at the beginning of the school year, however the organization of the infant department differed. In one there were two reception classes. In the other there were four family-grouped classes, each with first- and second-year children; only two of these four classes were included in the research. The smaller size of the other three schools (each with an intake of around 40 children during the year), combined with three entry dates with unequal proportions of children entering on the various entry dates, resulted in changes of class for 34 of these children during their first year in school. By the end of the school year 19 children had already left these five schools.

Thus the first year in primary school would have been very different for the children in this study: their age on entry, the age range of the class and whether they remained in the same class with their friends for their first year in school. For the teachers, all of whom were teaching 'reception class', the characteristics of the children would also have been very different.

> Consider how many variables have been identified already which may influence children's early learning experiences, even in a relatively small sample such as this. We have not yet considered the context of the classroom or the methods adopted by the individual teachers.

The children's preschool experiences had also differed: some were already attending the primary school's nursery class, others entered with friends from a nearby preschool unit, others as strangers to their classmates.

LANGUAGE ASSESSMENT OF CHILDREN IN A VARIETY OF SETTINGS

The communication skills of the children were assessed in a variety of ways, with peers and with their teachers. Some assessment was in 'contrived' situations, to ensure that the more-able children were 'stretched', possibly beyond what might have been available to them in the naturally occurring settings, and children with difficulties were given an opportunity to show their competence when the demands were quite specifically tailored.

By test

It was planned to select 'target' children in the reception classes as the focus for the language aspect of the research. Children from different ethnic minorities for whom we already had samples of language from the preschool unit were chosen, with additional children who had entered reception class direct from home. As these children were in five different schools it was important to have some assessment of their language on a common measure. Initially it was intended to test only these children. Subsequently it was decided to undertake the considerable additional work so that results on the test would be available for all children in the reception classes. Thus we had some idea of how comparable was the range of competence with which the various reception class teachers were faced in terms of the children's understanding of English on entering the class. We were also able to compare the range of competence within the different ethnic groupings.

Another decision we made after the start of the research was to test all the children whose mother tongue was Punjabi not only in English, but also in their mother tongue. This was feasible because one of my students had Punjabi as her mother tongue (see Whittaker 1985 for full details of this assessment). In their second year these children were then retested in English to assess the extent of progress made by the low scoring children during their first year in school. It was appreciated that even with several months between repeat testing, use of the same test again meant that practice with the test might well explain some of the improvement in children's scores; nevertheless the advantages in using the same test were felt in this instance to outweigh any disadvantages.

A decision had to be taken on what language test to use with such young children. The language tests popular in the 1960s and 1970s are less frequently used now, with a growing reluctance to use psychometric tests with young children. The work with preschool children of an American psychologist, Marion Blank, during and after the Head Start projects in the United States, had come to my attention, and in particular her Preschool Language Assessment Instrument (PLAI) which seemed ideal for the purposes of this research (Blank, Rose and Berlin 1978a; 1978b). We had used it and found it valuable with the pairs of children with special needs and their controls in an earlier study, where we used it in association with the analysis Marion Blank devised for the assessment of natural discourse between young children or between them and adults (see Robson 1989). PLAI is still cited in more recent research (Broadhead 1996, for example).

PLAI was devised specifically for children about this age, at the point of entry to school, and consists of 15 questions at each of four levels of complexity, chosen to reflect the type of questions faced in the classroom. The levels involve:

- matching perception
- selective analysis of perceptions
- reordering perception
- reasoning about perception.

These are assessed in ways to which young children should be able to respond by 4 or 5 years of age.

The test materials consist of line drawings, and most questions require only pointing or a few words for an adequate response, even for higher levels of questions, although some of these latter questions do require verbal answers. In this way it is possible to assess a child's *comprehension of language* separated as far as possible from the child's ability to *communicate in language*, an important distinction. Valuable diagnostic information can be obtained not only from a study of the children's scores for each level of questions, but also from an analysis of their errors. These are categorized as:

- ambiguous
- inadequate
- irrelevant.

How frequently they say 'don't know', or remain silent is also considered.

> You could gain important insights from an analysis of children's responses to questions to which they do not give the correct answer. Do they tend to give an answer which is nearly correct, to guess (even wildly), to say they 'don't know' or to remain silent? How can you encourage them to give you sufficient clues to be able to help them?

For clarity, an example is given below of a question on each level of difficulty in PLAI and some acceptable answers:

Level 1:   What is the lady doing? (*picture shown*)
            a Drinking
            b Drinking her tea

Level 2:   Look at these, how are they different? (picture shown)
            a One's got stabilizers, that one's for a big kid and that one's for a small kid
            b Two wheeler and three wheeler

Level 3:   A lady went into a supermarket and saw something which was not food. What could she have seen?
            a She could have seen a clock
            b Some children

Level 4:   If the circle were made of this colour instead of this colour would it still be a circle? Why? (picture shown)
            a Yes, because it would still be round
            b Yes, because it's already a circle

A decision had to be made concerning when to test the children who, it will be remembered, differed widely in age on entry to school (from about 4 to 5 years of age).

One option was to test the children as they reached the same age; the alternative was to test each child near the point of entry to school. This latter option was chosen, reflecting as it did the children's competence as presented to the reception class teacher initially. It was possible to test 215 of the 247 children in the reception classes on PLAI; most of those omitted were late entries to school or left that school before they could be tested.

> When studying researches you should check how many of the sample are *not* included in the results and whether reasons are given for their omission. It becomes progressively more time-consuming to 'catch' the last few children in a class, yet, as should be appreciated, among this group with less regular attendance may be some of these children with the greatest problems.

As might have been expected, a number of the low-scoring children on the test were among the youngest in the sample. It is important to stress, however, that in *each of these schools* there were some children entering reception class who had impressive abilities and who understood and responded to questions of high levels of complexity and perceptual distance. There were other children in each school who were able only to respond appropriately to simple questions tied closely to perception. Furthermore, even when assessed in

English, there were *within each ethnic group* children who were able to answer appropriately questions on all four levels of difficulty. Likewise, there were children from each ethnic background with very limited understanding of anything beyond simple labelling questions.

Although most of the children for whom Punjabi was their mother tongue were able to respond to the test when PLAI was presented in that language, there was a wide range of competence in their mother tongue. There were indeed some children who had severe difficulty in coping with demands such as these even in their mother tongue – a difficulty which might well not have been appreciated by their teacher if she did not speak the children's language and had no access to such assessments. Such information has important educational implications. It is a very much simpler cognitive task to understand concepts in a second language if they are already fully appreciated in a first language.

Equally important was the finding that there were some young children who had impressive competence in *both* English and Punjabi. This we were able to show not only on test performance captured on video, but also in dialogue between peers that we recorded.

Teachers' judgements

There are dangers in overestimating children's understanding of language as there are in underestimating it. It therefore seemed worthwhile to devise sample questions paralleling the levels of complexity on PLAI, and ask the reception class teachers to make a judgement on which of their children they would expect to answer each question successfully.

Arrangements were made to free the teacher so that she could be interviewed away from her class (by volunteering to take her class). It may be useful to describe the procedure which we adopted (which was intended to avoid the 'halo effect'), which leads a person who regards a child as good or bad, weak or strong, to score each question in a comparable way, irrespective of the question.

As each question in turn was shown to the teacher, printed on a separate card, the names of the children in the class were read out in alphabetic order (boys and girls interspersed). For the first two simpler questions the teacher was asked to indicate any child she thought would not answer correctly. The researcher then placed a cross at the appropriate children's names (the teacher could not see the responses and was therefore less likely to be influenced for the next question). For each of the remaining two harder questions, to avoid 'response set' the teacher was asked to indicate for each child if he or she would answer correctly.

The limitations of this brief test should be obvious were it to be treated in isolation. Here, however, it formed part of a picture of children's competence and teacher perception that was being built up over a period of time and on a variety of tasks. It did reveal some interesting differences in the teachers' perceptions of the range of competence in their class, and the abilities of individual children, including children who we had found on the test to respond in a very similar way.

Teacher–child dialogue

A further way in which samples of language were collected was by recording teacher-initiated dialogue in the classroom with individual children for whom samples of language were already available. Each teacher was asked, while wearing a radio microphone, to speak with the selected children one-to-one for a few minutes in such a way as to show the children's dialogue skills, 'stretching' the children to show the limits of their ability. Included in this sample were children who had scored high on PLAI and others who had extreme difficulty. Twenty-five of these children were among 44 subsequently recorded in dialogue with groups of peers in a planned setting. This task showed that teachers adopted very different styles of questioning. Some demonstrated more successful strategies in drawing out responses from the children; other strategies resulted in limited or single word responses from the children.

We found that when talking to the children in a one-to-one situation the teachers were inclined to use questions to excess to initiate and sustain dialogue, and to use questions which varied little in their level of complexity. Their questions often required certain types of labelling and frequently one- or two-word answers. Such questions we observed often failed to stretch children who we knew to be more able conversationalists. On occasion confusion was caused to the less-able where strings of such questions were used.

Three examples of such 'strings', of which there were many, are as follows:

Example 1:
Teacher: A doll? Have you got lots of dolls at home? And what are their names? Have you got names for them?
Child: Yes.

Example 2:
Teacher: Is he a big brother? Is he your big brother? Doesn't he play in the band at school? Does he? Where does he play? Do you know the name of the instrument?
Child: (Shakes his head)

Example 3:
Teacher: Was it lovely? Was it hot there? Was it hot? Did you wear warm clothes like this? What did you wear?
Child: Shorts.

The first example is from dialogue with a less-able child who found these multiple questions difficult, particularly as it was a frequently used strategy. The other two examples are from discussion with more-able children, for one of whom English was a second language.

Another tendency was to ask forced choice questions, such as: 'Did you come back on the same day or another day?' or 'Do you think they're hiding or looking for something?'

Some of these teachers were concerned when they realized the style they had adopted and its effects. They discovered that if they adopted a different strategy and a more conversational style they could develop an interesting dialogue with a number of the children. Even some of the more-able conversationalists among the teachers were horrified at the number of questions they asked, and the type of questions (see also Chapter 5).

> You may feel you would not fall into such a trap, but record yourself attempting to elicit conversation from a young child who is a stranger to you, especially a shy child. This was a practical I set my students, most of whom were already experienced teachers, although some had not worked with young children. On occasion the results were revealing to them, and embarrassing!

We did find that some of the teachers adopted successful strategies which encouraged the more-able children to respond beyond the questions asked, thereby the discussion flowed and was extended. The skilled conversationalist, whether adult or child, has the ability to encourage others to explore and extend their ideas, not only by questions which lead to further development of a theme, but also by related comments and a demonstrated interest in the concerns of others. This may be apparent in pacing of interjections – and even in silences long enough for the other person to continue and expand a theme! This latter point is worthy of study in the classroom, namely the 'wait time' allowed by a teacher after posing a question, and how that varies for different children. A teacher may actually wait less, not more time when asking a question of a less-able child (see Katz 1985 and Blank 1985).

> This would be interesting for you to study in a variety of situations, in classrooms and elsewhere. Observe what questions are asked; who is called upon to answer, and how frequently; how long is a silence tolerated in general before someone else is called upon; how great is the variation in the length of pauses? Not least, how different, and in what direction, is the variation for the more-competent and less-competent children?

Language in a variety of natural settings

Recordings were made of the conversations of selected children in a number of settings.

Recordings in preschool units

Samples of language in the two nursery schools and three nursery classes were made for 25 children shortly before their transfer to reception class, using radio microphones and a format similar to that used in the research on children with special needs (Robson 1983a; 1983b; 1989). The recordings, which were made during free play, varied in length from 20 to 45 minutes and included discussion between peers and with adults. During the recording the target child could move freely around the unit; an observer unobtrusively noted context details to help with the analysis of the recordings.

These samples of language for target children could be compared with the children's language in other settings when they entered primary school. They also provided insights on more-successful or less-successful settings and activities within the preschool units and concerning strategies adopted by the adults to encourage children to contribute. The head teacher of one of the nursery schools, who became one of my students, was able to analyse the transcripts from that point of view for her dissertation (see Payne 1985).

The fact that children's language was assessed and recorded in a variety of settings, and over time, made it possible to appreciate the influence of a number of these variables, and not least *how dangerous it would be to attempt to assess a child's communicative competence from only one sample of language, or even one type of setting* (see *Helping Communication in Early Education*, Clark 1985a). This point can perhaps best be illustrated by the following example from one of the recordings in a preschool unit.

Child 1:   It's time to do the washing now.
           (She pretends to wash doll's clothes alongside peer)
           Well! How many! What a lot of clothes I'm going to wash, and there are so many more yet.
Child 2:   Haven't you finished the washing yet?
Child 1:   We're just going to wash, I'll do it, I'll wash.
           (Child 1 sorts the washing)
           This is dirty and this is clean.
           It's not warm *(feels the water)*. It's cold.
           I'm going to warm the water first because they're really dirty.
           (Continued with baby on Child 1's lap sitting at table with peer and baby)
Child 1:   Oh look your baby's mouth is open!
Child 3:   You sit down and have your food.
Child 1:   Yes I'll sit down and have my food, I'm not going to put this on the baby because it's dirty *(dress)*
Child 3:   Don't you want to eat your food?
Child 1:   I've just put it on her and she has taken it off!
(This dialogue was continued and extended involving other children)

This extract has been quoted at some length and it was tempting to quote even more as it continued to be complex, imaginative with extended role-playing which involved a number of children, sustained by Child 1. I have chosen this example because the child in question was not yet 4 years of age; furthermore she and her companions were discussing in Punjabi, their mother tongue. This is a translation from a tape. The privacy and freedom to use her mother tongue were essential for this play to have taken place, as this child at this stage had little English, and in other settings was shy, rather withdrawn and answered with only the odd word. She was later supported in the reception class into communicating in English partly by structured play situations with a language focus and by outside visits organized by the ethnic support team to encourage her to use English. The importance for this child of an opportunity to play in this setting was clear, as was the need to see her in settings such as this, if one were not to underestimate her abilities.

There was evidence of differences in the extent to which children were at ease and communicative with different adults, and adults with different children. Very apparent from these recordings from preschool units was the importance of organization skills, choice of activities and the adult's approach to the children, if the maximum benefit was to be gained by all the children.

Recordings in reception classrooms

Opportunities for dialogue depended not just on the abilities of the children but on the layout of the classroom, whether this facilitated or allowed them to explore, interact and choose their own activities on occasion within social settings. The 'home corner' (with dressing up materials), painting and sand, and building materials all helped. Time was also required for absorbing play to develop, to make something or communicate to a real audience. One child with little English was encouraged to use Punjabi and, with peers in the home corner, organize an assembly, later presented to the whole class. A flexible but structured timetable was necessary for such experiences to occur. Even children with language difficulties were seen to attempt communication in some settings.

Example 1:   The children are sticking material to make a reindeer.
Child 1:   (approaching the table) What are you making?
Child 2:   We're making reindeer.
Child 3:   Yes, we're making. . . (continues to stick with gusto)
Child 2:   Oh that girl is coming in here! (adult comes in through the archway)
Child 3:   That's not her, that's Mrs—
Child 4:   She was coming in here.
Child 3:   I never saw her.
Child 4:   (teasing) Oh you!

Imitation of one's peers, especially by children such as Child 3 above, striving to communicate, was apparent throughout the recordings.

Example 2:   While concentrating on a variety of activities, Child 2, who had recently entered reception class straight from abroad, managed some interaction in spite of his limited communication skills. He gained support from the teacher and his classmates both in examples such as this and in the playground.

Child 1:   (Is copying script above something he has drawn)
Child 2:   New book, I've got no clean pages. What's that? (points to the drawing)
Child 1:   Same as mine. Looks like a big man.
Child 2:   Ain't got no yellow, have you?
Child 1:   You can have a big one. I'll have a little one. You have to have one of those don't you. You're naughty . . . same as me!
(Child 1's utterances are interspersed with hums and snatches of song)

The teacher controlled this group, which continued for 25 minutes, during which she allowed initiations between the children, yet ensured they kept to the task.

In another instance a group of children was absorbed in physical activities, while fringe peers were drawn into the play – except for one child who, when she attempted to join in, was met with: 'Who said you can play?'

We found this child to have problems in being accepted in numerous settings, in the playground and also in the group discussions we planned. She had poor language and appeared helpless in face of these rebuffs. Our evidence drew attention to just how serious were her difficulties.

Recordings were made in only one of the ethnic support settings, where there was a large enough classroom for the observer to remain relatively unobtrusive. There the curriculum was activity-based and the children were gradually encouraged to respond in English.

Many examples from reception classrooms could be given where conversation was sustained by two or more children. Encouragement or permission to converse appeared to prolong the concentration rather than distract from the task in hand. There were occasions of course in all classrooms where silence or quietness was regarded as essential for work, or where group interaction was regarded as play. In these latter settings there were only limited opportunities for children to share experiences; communication was likely to be limited, and only with an adult or to a larger group of children in response to teacher questioning. The contexts provided in the different classrooms will be considered in Chapter 9, as will be the views of the teachers and some of the parents on early education.

Playgrounds as settings for dialogue

Able children were seen to devise their own settings for interaction on an abstract, fantasy game level. Features of such language were its spontaneity, the use of rhythm and song, recognition of the abilities of peers and like-minded friendship groupings. Some of the recordings mirrored what had been found in outside play areas in the preschool units. Close, but unobtrusive, adult supervision and intervention yielded opportunities for dialogue. The layout of the playground was significant in encouraging dynamic play; though in some less-promising settings it was also possible to record examples of interesting conversations. In the playgrounds some of those with difficulties were able to let off steam. However, we observed that for a few, playtime seemed a stressful time, and dinner time even worse. A change that occurred in one school after the research was that the play area for the younger children was separated, where previously they had to face the presence of the older children in the same large area.

Group discussions between young children

This aspect of the project, which took place when the children were around 5 years of age and involved a 'contrived' situation planned to stimulate discussion among the children, was the idea of one of my students who used such a strategy in her own reception classroom. She wanted to undertake such a project as part of her coursework. It was to our mutual benefit that she involved children within the research sample for whom other information was already available (see Coates 1985). The children in groups of four were provided with a tray of interesting objects, which it was hoped would stimulate conversation and co-operation. On the tray were the following: a torch in working order, a torch complete but in pieces, a set of colour paddles and a colour pyramid.

The children were initially left to explore these by themselves; later they were joined by an adult who then took part in the discussion. A radio microphone was used to record the dialogue. To assist subsequent analysis, a researcher sitting at a distance noted the names of the children who were contributing and any other relevant points. This aspect of the research included 44 of the 215 children who had been assessed on PLAI, and as many children as possible for whom samples of language in other settings were available.

It was decided to have only four children in each group, as this had been found to be the maximum number whose voices could be identified subsequently during transcription of the recordings. All four children in a group were from the same school, and usually the same class. Each group had at least one child from an ethnic minority background, and within each group was one more-able, one less-able and two average children, as assessed on PLAI. The groups were not matched for ability or sex balance; indeed if you consider the problems any attempt at matching within and between schools would have presented, the impossibility of achieving matched groups within a sample such as this will be apparent. This limitation was recognized when analysing the ensuing discussions.

In spite of the problems encountered and the limitations in the sample, a number of interesting findings of importance to early education were identified, not least the competence of these young children to engage in dialogue with peers when provided with sufficiently challenging and stimulating materials. It should be remembered that the children were around 5 years of age, for at least one child in each group the mother tongue was not English and that there was a range of language ability in each group. Initially there was no adult guidance or intervention.

Among the measures which were considered were:

- numbers of turns taken by the various members of the group
- numbers of complex sentences
- differences in the dialogue before and after the arrival of the adult.

The following are interesting findings from the study:

- The objects chosen stimulated the children to explore and discuss. The two torches, one in pieces, challenged the children to make that one work. The colour paddles and pyramid resulted in lots of discussion on colour and magic. Sometimes the paddles or pyramid were used in conjunction with the torch, to the excitement of the children.
- Most children shared in turn-taking and, before the adult joined the group, in most groups the children already had between 30 and 40 turns each.
- Contributions of more than one sentence in length were made by many of the more-able children, and by children from each ethnic minority background. Two of these young children for whom English was a second language (the mother tongue of one was Punjabi, the other Gujerati) contributed to the child–child dialogue in different groups in an animated interesting and knowledgeable way, including over 30 turns each of more than one sentence in length.
- After the adult joined the group, most of the children's utterances tended to be shorter, and the children deferred to the adult as leader. A number of the utterances were quite complex, however, as the children attempted to report previously experienced activities to the adult. It should be noted that the children were not aware that the adult had any conception of their prior discussions. The adult discovered to her embarrassment that she, although an experienced teacher of young

children, had found it difficult not to dominate the groups with numerous questions!

It is important to consider both quantity and quality of talk, and this was done in the analysis. In the research report examples are given of 16 consecutive turns from six of the groups, illustrating the contributions of the various children, and that a real dialogue was taking place in this context, in spite of the limitations in the surface features of some of the children's language and the reticence of some in adult–child dialogue recorded in other settings (see also Coates 1985). In this chapter the flavour of the discussions will be given through illustrations from two groups. It is important to know what was happening as well as what was being said. The interactions in this first group are typical of most of the groups, with sometimes discussion in pairs, or one child showing another something exciting, or one acting as leader for part of the time.

Example 1:   Before the adult joined the group, the children had 14, 36, 36 and 33 turns respectively. This extract is taken from near the beginning.

Leanne: Can't get it back on. I can't get it back on.

Keith: Is there a battery in that?
          (short pause)

Rajan: I know where dis work.
          (Rajan explains how he thinks it works by pointing at different parts)
          When this touch dat, then it works. Look it's touching it!

Barbara: How it works?

Rajan: Yes, I'll tell you what I mean.
          (Rajan hasn't managed to put it back together yet)
          Look, see that battery. Find the other battery first. If you do that then it works.

Keith: What do you do?

Leanne: I don't know.

Keith: I want this.
          (He picks up the paddles)
          I can see a red Leanne. Can you Barbara?
          (Barbara looks through as well)

Barbara: I can see a red S—.

Rajan: Here! This is how it works. When this hole touch that, then it works.

Example 2:   In the child–child dialogue there were turns by all four children 28, 35, 32 and 17 respectively before the adult joined the group. In this group the first three children were interacting in an excited and stimulating way. However attempts by the fourth child (child 1) to obtain either a share of the materials or to be included in the discussion continued to be rejected.

Child 1:   I want a torch
Child 2:   You're not having this one though. You're having T's torch.
Child 1:   Can't I have a little try. I want a torch.
Child 2:   You're not having mine.
(Shortly after she tries to attract attention by showing colour paddles but others ignore her)

While a different grouping, or earlier adult intervention, might have helped this child to be accepted, this simple alternative is unlikely to have solved her difficulties. We know from other recordings that her language was limited and that she tended to be rejected in other settings also, including the playground.

COMMENTS

The reception class teachers were committed to providing the children with planned and systematically presented instruction in the basic skills from an early stage. They were not all fully aware of the contexts for language development that had been provided in the preschool units, or even that this was an important goal in these units. There was a tendency for some of these teachers to assume that extended dialogue for these young children was either not possible, or required the involvement at all stages of an adult, as instructor and initiator also. As I have indicated we found many examples of these young children in animated conversation in a variety of settings.

> You could gain valuable insights by recording children's language in a variety of settings with and without adult support and intervention. Remember to ask permission from the children as well as the adults.

In the following chapter I will consider the reception classrooms as contexts for learning and the views of the teachers and of the parents.

Chapter 9

Reception classrooms as contexts for learning

Part 2 of a DES-funded study

BACKGROUND

In the previous chapter the language of young children who entered reception class in five primary schools in England with varied proportions of children from different ethnic minorities was discussed. The evidence was taken from a DES-funded research which I directed. The samples of language were from preschool units, reception classes and the playground. In this chapter I will consider reception classrooms as contexts for learning, based on observations in each classroom and on evidence from interviews with staff, promoted staff, Ethnic Minority Support Service and the parents of some of the children. At least by implication, assumptions are often made about the aims and priorities of teachers and features which are thought to facilitate or constrain their achievement. It seemed important to explore the views of the teachers on topics related to early education. An extension of the research made this possible immediately after the children in the study had completed their time in the reception class. The extension also enabled us to interview selected parents in their mother tongue in their homes. In addition, a number of my students were able to utilize the schedules we developed during the research for their dissertations.

RECEPTION CLASSROOMS

The children

Learning in school takes place in a social context; this includes a large number of children of about the same age whose competing needs must be met by the teacher. A particular child's adjustment to school and their progress and range of learning will be influenced by the skills and characteristics of classmates as well as by the curriculum, teaching style and personality of the teacher.

While the focus here is on the similarities and differences in the classrooms, the different characteristics, even age ranges of the children in these classrooms, must be remembered. In some of these classrooms a child might be one of only a few with limited command of English on entry; in other classrooms such children had companions with whom they were able to communicate. The child who is socially acceptable, even if under stress and of limited language competence, may be supported by his or her classmates both in the classroom and in the playground. Some children demand, and receive, greater attention than others; some more reticent or less socially acceptable, to adults as well as children, may succeed only rarely in obtaining extended attention from the teacher. The teacher in the busy setting of the classroom, with such varied demands, as we found, seldom has an opportunity for extended dialogue with children. Furthermore, that attention is differentially shared among the children; some whose need is greatest may receive little individual attention.

> Before reading this chapter, in your order of priority list the aims of teachers of young children. By observation of target children, study the way the teacher's attention is shared across the children. Perhaps choose older and younger children, or children the teacher expected to succeed, or others for whom difficulties were anticipated. Remember to include boys and girls. It would be helpful to do your observations with a friend. You might be surprised at how differently reality is viewed from different perspectives.

The schools

External constraints determine to some extent not only what is taught, but also the way in which the day is organized. National curricular guidelines, local authority recommendations and, not least, the age of the children on entry to reception class, or any class, will all play their part. As was noted earlier, the organization of the school will be influenced by the size of school, by the size of intake and whether there is more than one intake per year. Likewise, staff with special responsibility within the school will influence the way the curriculum is presented and the resources, in terms of teaching assistants and materials, available in the classroom. They will decide whether materials are held centrally or within individual classrooms. In two of the schools there were members of the Ethnic Minority Support Service (EMSS); in both schools the support was by withdrawal from the classroom – not the decision of the class teachers, but something which must have affected timetabling. As was noted earlier, in this research there were nine classrooms with reception age children; in three of the schools there was only one reception class, in one large school there were two reception classes and in the remaining school there were four classes which had both reception age children and older children. We found not only differences between schools but also between classrooms in the same school.

Profiles of the classrooms

Three visits were made to each of the seven classrooms where we had observed children. On each occasion a diagrammatic sketch was made showing the location of the furniture, the equipment, the place of the teacher's desk, height of display boards, siting of the home corner, paints, etc. We observed how much the layout varied over time, and also how much the children contributed to wall displays, for example, and how much these reflected the multicultural characteristics of the children. We also observed in the settings used by the EMSS teachers.

We found the categories used in the researches on transition discussed in Chapter 7 helpful in differentiating the classrooms and teaching styles; one example was the *play/work dichotomy*. In some instances 'play' became either what you did in nursery school but don't do in 'big school', except at play-time, or what you do after you have finished your work. How constrained was the *choice of activities*, and for how much of the day this was permitted, were important. In the preschools some children had been given the opportunity to concentrate on chosen activities for long periods. However, others faced with unlimited choice, perhaps not knowing how to play, having limited language or being unacceptable to other children, could benefit from more structure than was common in some preschool units at that time.

In a previous research in which we observed in large open-plan nursery schools we found that some children in a free play atmosphere remained on the fringe of activities and became 'drifters' (see Clark and Cheyne 1979). The layout of the classrooms in the present study revealed the extent to which the teachers encouraged *mobility in the classroom*, a feature we had observed in the preschool units. A further aspect we compared, seen both from layout and timetabling, was the extent to which the teachers encouraged *independence* and *child initiation*. Differences in the extent to which the teachers perceived the children as initiators and encouraged movement were reflected in the grouping of desks, placement of equipment and the height and contents of the display boards. We also observed differences in permitted noise level, and whether the children were encouraged to interact with others if this was not distracting; with some teachers this was less in evidence. When we interviewed the teachers we confirmed from their answers a number of observations we had made earlier on the classroom organization.

All the teachers in our study were experienced, committed teachers who nonetheless had characteristically different patterns of organization of the rooms, also reflected in other aspects of their teaching. All seven teachers had general timetables; some had more specific timetables; some offered an element of choice. In most cases careful records were kept of precisely where each child had reached on a given aspect of their work. A general distinction we found valuable in differentiating classrooms and teaching style was between the teachers who saw themselves as *counsellor* and those who saw themselves as *instructor*. This was used to great effect by Southgate and Roberts, reported in *Reading – Which Approach?* (1970). In some of the schools the day was consciously teacher-directed and also more work-orientated. The extent of the teacher's talk, to whom she talked and about what seemed influenced by her general style of teaching, as was how the children were grouped. This was linked to whether the teachers saw the pupils as initiators as well as respondents, or whether the learning environment was subject to greater social control and teacher-dependent activities.

The pattern of the day as well as the organization of the learning activities appeared to be rather different depending on the teacher's style, whether counsellor or instructor. The counsellor teacher tended to balance teacher-dependent and/or supervised activities alongside free choice play activities over the day and week. In contrast, the instructor style of teaching placed priority on teacher-directed activities in the morning relating to the 3Rs and more creative but teacher-chosen activities in the afternoon.

One of the research team, Wendy Dewhirst, used this distinction in looking at examples of the dialogue we obtained from the children in the different settings (Dewhirst 1985). She pointed out that in classrooms in which the teacher revealed a counsellor style, many of the settings available to the children still mirrored those we found in preschool units, and the dialogue recorded similar patterns of peer group interaction. Children we followed from preschool units into these settings made easier transitions into school, settling into the pattern of the day in a relatively positive and relaxed manner. Such settings also enabled children without experience of a preschool unit, those coming from home or overseas, and the late entrants, to make relatively easier adjustment. This ethos and organization enabled them to interact or withdraw into a variety of settings offering security, interest and friendship. In one classroom for example some children for whom Punjabi was their mother tongue were grouped together and permitted to talk together in their mother tongue, even although it was not understood by the teacher. In the instructor style classrooms the demands of teacher-directed activities frequently limited the dialogue between children, particularly in the mornings. The aims of the teachers and the curriculum will be considered later in this chapter, based on evidence from the teacher interviews.

Other adults in the classroom

In addition to the teacher there was in each of the classrooms at least one other adult available for part of the day – a nursery nurse or helper, often shared with other classes. There were differences in the extent to which the planning for the day was made explicit to the assistants. In one classroom information on activities for the week was displayed for the benefit of the other adults. In one school there were young adults from ethnic minorities who had been recruited under the Manpower Services Scheme and who were encouraged to talk with the children (where appropriate in their mother tongue). More than one young girl in that school as a result of that experience decided to train as a nursery nurse. There was little evidence in any of the classrooms of parents being in the classroom on a regular basis, although there might be close links with some mothers. However, there was evidence during the research of a great deal of community involvement in several of the schools. A member of the research team prepared a video for the school of one such occasion.

EMSS classrooms

Two of the large schools, in which English was a second language for many of the children, had members of the EMSS based in the school; selected children were helped on a withdrawal basis.

In one of these schools a large classroom was allocated to two of these teachers, who worked together with groups of about 12 children. The selected children attended each day, and this was arranged in collaboration with the head of the infant department and the reception class teachers. A balance of activities was provided, with the aim that the regular teacher and EMSS teacher should support each other. The teachers conversed with the children, then refined question demands to assist the children in developing competence in English. This was supported by stories, concrete and creative activities and shopping expeditions. These teachers would have appreciated time to visit the homes of some of these children.

In the other school, only a small room was available, and that teacher arranged her timetable in a more flexible way with small groups of children for sessions of 10–15 minutes. The room was attractive, with a range of pictorial materials and multi-ethnic characters. This teacher did not have the support of a second teacher. The children we observed in this room clearly enjoyed the structured setting and the innovative approach that was used with the materials. We did not observe in the other room as there was a relief teacher there at the time.

We became aware in the course of our research how the withdrawal system impacted on the reception class teachers' planning for the basic skills and other aspects of the curriculum. During the interviews we sought their views on this.

> Controversy surrounds the best approach to providing additional help for children with limited language, or indeed with reading difficulties. Some may favour withdrawal on a regular basis; others, aware of the disruption it causes to the teacher in the main classroom, feel the disadvantages outweigh any

benefits. Consider the advantages and disadvantages of each approach for the staff involved, and for the children.

INTERVIEWS OF RECEPTION CLASS TEACHERS

The questions

The interviews were carefully planned, and all were conducted by the same interviewer in a relaxed atmosphere away from the pressures of the classroom, while a member of the research team took responsibility for the class. The teacher in charge of the infant department in two of the schools was also interviewed, the two schools being those with more than one reception class and a nursery class. The members of the EMSS staff in these two schools, who had worked with children in our study, were also interviewed. Some questions concerned named children who had been in the reception class during the research, and about whom we already knew a great deal. As the interviews progressed the teachers were asked about their aims and priorities at greater levels of specificity to ensure that both the teachers' spontaneously expressed priorities and specific aspects of the curriculum and organization were covered during the interview.

Questions were also asked about the range of skills the children were felt to have brought with them and what the teachers hoped to achieve with most children during their time in reception class. This was then related to children who had or did not have prior experience in a preschool unit. Specific questions were then asked with particular reference to the basic skills, and the extent to which the reception class teachers felt constrained by the expectations of others, colleagues or parents.

Teachers were asked how their aims would be modified for children with particular difficulties, or children who were outstanding. Differences in aims between preschool educators and reception classes were explored, as perceived by these teachers.

Although all classes had some children from ethnic minorities, specific reference was not made to these in the questions in the early part of the interview, only later when the teachers had been given an opportunity to make spontaneous comments.

Finally, the teachers were given an opportunity to raise points not covered in the interview that they felt to be important.

It is important to note that we were working with a small number of schools, five only, and nine reception class teachers, the promoted staff in the schools and the teachers from the EMSS. Had there been a large sample we would have prepared a much more structured interview schedule, and piloted it first. By the time we interviewed the teachers we knew them well, and knew a great deal about their classroom practices and the children's ability. Finally the interviews were all conducted by the same interviewer, who was well-known to the teachers and an expert on early education.

You might find it valuable to draw up your own schedule for such an interview and to consider what responses you would anticipate from teachers. Compare your schedule with the one used here with reception class teachers (see Appendix 1).

The answers

Aims and priorities

Questions related to aims were interspersed throughout the interview, the first was most general, later questions related to specific aspects of the curriculum. In answer to the general question, most of the teachers responded with some comments about settling the children into school, using words such as 'making the children secure' or 'having good attitudes to work'. The importance of language was mentioned by several teachers in relation to getting the children prepared for the basic skills or 'to develop the academic levels for which they were capable'. Several teachers referred to material aspects, such as a large classroom enabling the children to move around; others mentioned human resources, such as the prevailing atmosphere in the school and the involvement of the parents. Constraining features noted included the difference between children who had come from nursery classes and those who had come straight from home. The need for more time from nursery nurses was also mentioned.

It is worth noting that in spite of the very different age range of 'reception' children in the different schools, only one teacher mentioned age differences as being a problem. We expected some reference to be made to how different might be the age range of children in reception class. The teacher who did comment was one with a family-grouped classroom, who found herself torn between the need for the younger children to play and the need for older children to work.

One teacher referring to the children's limited concentration and skills as constraints later commented that she might have attempted to advance the children too much (it was her first year teaching reception class). Another teacher noted that she would do things differently next year; she would attempt to show more patience initially, allowing more time settling the children. She said she had been 'guilty of trying to teach with a big T'.

Bear in mind that this research was conducted in the 1980s in England, before the introduction of the National Curriculum, SATs and the literacy and numeracy hours. Consider how these might have changed teachers' priorities for the early years in primary school.

From their answers it was clear that the basic skills were important to these teachers. Most introduced reading with the assistance of Breakthrough to Literacy, which they regarded as a valuable resource in connection with productive writing. Reference was also made to phonics and flashcards. Several teachers did comment on the value of story reading as a stimulus to the imagination, to oral language development or as a relaxed end to the day. One teacher said she had given the children a book straight away, another commented that she had perhaps given the children a book too soon. The teachers regarded the resources for teaching reading as adequate, though several stressed the time pressures in hearing all the children reading. In answer to the question about the early stages of writing, it appeared that the teachers interpreted this as referring to handwriting, not to producing written language, until this was specifically asked. Thus their answers were about tracing and copying, pattern making and ensuring that the children did not develop bad habits. Surprisingly there were no references to the wide age ranges within some classes, which would surely have resulted in very different levels of motor co-ordination. These answers do not appear to be an artefact of the questions, as this was reflected in the observations in the classrooms and in the samples of children's writing collected during the study.

With reference to number work most teachers referred to Nuffield mathematics and specific mention was made of matching, sorting and correspondence.

Range of skills

According to several teachers the range of skills brought by the children was 'vast', examples were given of named children. Several teachers indicated that they would mix groups to include the more- and less-advanced; most referred to teaching materials or talking with the children. Some teachers felt they had been too anxious to advance the children; 'too conscious of accelerating their skills' and 'didn't allow enough play'. One of these teachers commented that the research had made her more aware of the children's levels.

All the teachers emphatically agreed that it was their responsibility to help overcome any language difficulties; 'it's part of my job', 'I get paid to do just that', 'it's part of my daily routine'. Surprisingly no teacher referred to the responsibility for oral language development being shared with an EMSS teacher in spite of the fact that six of the nine teachers interviewed had that support. Either this contribution was forgotten during the interview or was not fully appreciated. It is perhaps also surprising that no reference was made to problems caused by withdrawal of children from the classroom, which would have had organizational implications.

Pattern of intake

As has been indicated earlier, this was different in the various schools, it therefore seemed appropriate to discuss this issue in relation to the policy in that particular school. All the teachers who had only one intake preferred that organization as they felt the children were 'settled at once'. The three schools with three intakes were not happy with that arrangement; however, this was partly a reflection of the size of the groups and resultant change in class within a school year. They commented that 'you get to know the children just as they move up' or 'the summer intake always seems to lose out'. In the four classes with family grouping some advantages were mentioned, such as the older children helping settle the younger children. One teacher felt that she demanded too much of the younger children, who were expected to be quiet at times when she would have preferred to encourage more mobility.

Comparison of preschool and reception class

The responses of these teachers to questions about preschool education indicated that they regarded preschool education as socializing the children and teaching them to play. Most children in seven of the nine classes who had attended preschool education had attended a nursery class within that school. It was thus particularly surprising that these teachers had such limited know-ledge of the aims of preschool education. Few had visited the nursery class to see at first hand what range of activities was offered and the aims in these.

Most of the teachers referred to the need for structure, several indicating that mornings were structured for basic skills and afternoons for art and craft. These teachers tended to use expressions such as 'they can play when they have done their work' or ' play is still important, but I like them to get down to work'. Several, however, noted that 'play can be work disguised' or 'work is a teacher definition rather than a child's definition, they think it is a game'. The views expressed at interview on work and play did parallel what we had observed in the various classrooms, and were in accord with the findings of other researchers on differences in the views of preschool teachers and reception class teachers (see Chapter 7).

Children from ethnic minorities

No reference was made to children from ethnic minorities until towards the end of the interview; however, the teachers were already aware that this was a particular focus of the research. On studying the transcripts of the earlier part of the interviews we found that these teachers made few generalizations about children in terms of ethnic background. Occasional comments were made about problems for children for whom English was a second language, however teachers did stress that there were other children with difficulties.

There were virtually no references during the interviews to the Afro-Caribbean origin of any of the children; any reference was to specific children perceived as advanced or with difficulties.

Additional comments

The teachers seemed to feel that most points had been covered during the interview. Several stressed the need for more adults in the classroom to increase the children's experience of interaction. One teacher expressed a hope that they could get together and compare their aims; another hoped that something could be published to help them.

PROMOTED STAFF IN TWO SCHOOLS: THEIR CO-ORDINATING ROLE

In the two large schools there was more than one reception class, and also a nursery class that had been attended part-time by many of the children in our study. We sought the views of the promoted member of staff in each of these schools with responsibility for the infant department and nursery class. While the focus of the interviews was their co-ordinating role, most questions asked paralleled those asked of the reception class teachers.

In many ways their aims were similar; each gave a high priority to oral language development and stressed her role as facilitator in terms of information and resources. They also referred to the value of the EMSS teachers and the presence of nursery nurses; each stressed the need for enough adults in the classroom to enable work in small groups to take place. Their answers to questions on basic skills revealed the importance they placed on oral language as a basis for these skills. Reference was made to looking at books, talking about pictures and the need to move to reading through a variety of experiences. Story reading had a central role in their view, preferably as an interactive experience in small groups, introducing children to a wide range of literature. They both stressed the purpose of writing as well as the mechanical aspects, the need for children to be helped individually, to talk with an adult who could act as a scribe. The language of numbers, shopping and practical mathematics was mentioned. The views of these two promoted staff did not indicate that they set targets for the reception class which pressurized teachers into premature introduction of 'formal' work. The importance of viewing progress over the span of the infant department was noted. One of these staff, referring to constraints during the previous year, noted that she had at that time been teaching a class and that one of the EMSS teachers had been absent for much of the year.

These teachers were of course familiar with practice in preschool education as well as the infant department and had observed children making the transition. They commented on the problems with fewer adults in the infant classrooms and the possibility of a more leisurely pace in the nursery class. Both mentioned transition as a move to more structure and more group work rather than individual attention; both hoped there would still be opportunity for mobility and choice within the structure.

Their knowledge of the children who had attended nursery class was an important element in determining allocation to a particular reception class. They mentioned the differences between children direct from home, of whom there were few in these schools, and children from the nursery class, particularly in the first few weeks. Both teachers favoured a single entry date. Where they differed was that one was committed to family grouping, although she commented that she would have considered changing it had she felt the staff were unhappy with it.

Both staff showed a concern for the wide range of children in their care, and were articulate in their aims and sensitive as to the difficulties in translating these into practice. Both were aware that they could not impose their views on the staff for whom they were responsible. The importance of ensuring that the staff feel this work is worthwhile was the final point they stressed; that their staff do not feel the need to 'produce'.

VIEWS OF EMSS TEACHERS

The two large schools had high proportions of children for whom English was a second language. Each had teachers from the EMSS based in the school, helping selected children from the reception classes on a withdrawal basis. Three of these teachers were interviewed, the two who worked with small groups in a team-teaching setting, and one of the teachers in the other school.

Each of the teachers in the first school stated her aims in terms of helping the children's self-image, helping the children acquire a 'survival' language and linking between home and school. Neither saw it as her function to teach the children to read and write. In achieving their aims they said they structured play situations which would facilitate conversation. Neither would differentiate work and play, stressing the role of playing, arts and crafts and outside visits in developing communication. They felt that the children who had come through nursery class did not need as much of their support as those who had come straight from home.

It should be stressed that these two teachers were interviewed separately; thus the comparability of the views they expressed was not a consequence of the interview.

The teacher from the other large school also stressed language development as her aim, emphasizing the importance of having a room of her own where the context could be set and the quiet and diffident child encouraged. Among the constraints she noted were the absence of the other teacher for a long period and frequent absences of some of the children who needed most help. Long absences because of visits to India had affected some of the children, whom she felt had taken a considerable time to settle back into school. She noted that the range of skills of the children on entry was from virtually no English to a high level of competence. Like the other teachers she stressed the need for structure with occasional choice, and like them she felt that she taught through play. She expressed concern about a particular child who was making slow progress, appeared not to be coping in her mother tongue and did not even appear to speak to Punjabi-speaking peers.

PARENTS AND THEIR VIEWS

The sample and the interview

To complete this study it seemed important to obtain information on the perceptions of the parents; their expectations for their children and for early education. With our limited resources and timescale a selection had to be made of which parents to interview.

> Given limited resources, which parents would you have chosen, and what questions would you have asked?

The parents selected were those for whose children extensive language samples were available. Our knowledge of the children gave credibility to the interviews as the interviewer was seen by the parent(s) to be interested in, and knowledgeable about, the child. In view of the focus of the research we decided to interview mainly parents of children from ethnic minorities, with two exceptions. We added the parents of two able indigenous white children attending the same school as an able child of Afro-Caribbean origin, where we found these other parents could be free to attend on the same day. In another school three families of different ethnic origin were included for whom there were samples of language, where each child in the study had a younger sibling of the same sex and so close in age that the younger sibling had entered nursery school only a year later. These younger siblings were also assessed on PLAI, at about the same age, and interestingly were found to have relatively comparable scores to those of their older siblings at that age.

At least one parent of 23 of the children was interviewed:

- 11 of Asian ethnic origin (for 9 of whom Punjabi was the mother tongue)
- 9 of Afro-Caribbean origin
- 3 additional families referred to above.

Included were children from ethnic minority backgrounds with a wide range of language competence on entry to school (all had been assessed on PLAI on entry). Twenty of these children were among the 44 recorded in the group dialogue referred to in the previous chapter. By the time the interviews took place the children had been about two years in school.

Although it was important to have some structure and similarity in the interviews across ethnic background, a number of issues were pertinent to only one ethnic background. As the interviewers were not known to the parents, particular sensitivity was needed in deciding how far to explore family background and at what point in the interview to do so. Thus, the topics to be covered were decided in advance, and also questions to be asked where possible; the order of the questions, however, was left to the interviewer. See Appendix 2 for a list of the questions included in these interviews.

How different would your questions to parents be in the light of current educational priorities and changes in home circumstances?

The parents agreed that the interviews could be taped, which avoided excessive note taking during the interview; these were later transcribed for analysis. The nine parents whose mother tongue was Punjabi were interviewed at home, wholly or mainly in that language, by one of my students whose mother tongue was Punjabi and who already knew the children, having at an earlier stage tested them in their own language; she also translated the tapes. She managed to obtain a short study leave to undertake this work. The mother tongue of one of the other children of Asian ethnic origin was Gujerati, the other Bengali. I interviewed the father of one and the mother of the other. These parents were fluent enough in English for the interview to be conducted in that language. The remaining parents were interviewed either by Wendy Dewhirst or myself. Because of the relatively small sample of families, and their very different characteristics, we decided not to include case studies in the report, nor to include personal features which could have identified them. During the interviews we found the parents willing and interested to discuss their children, and we learnt a great deal about the complexity of life and the problems faced by so many of these parents.

Families of Asian ethnic origin

The interviews on which the following information is based were of both parents in three instances, of the mother in six and only the father in two. In all but one of the 11 families of Asian ethnic origin both parents were of similar ethnic background. In most of these homes the language spoken to each other by the adults was their mother tongue; this was also the language used to address the children. The parents reported that the children might address them in either their mother tongue or in English. All but one father had been at least

15 years in this country, and the mother in that family had been here longer. Not all the fathers were literate in their mother tongue; two had not attended school, others had limited schooling. Three of the mothers had arrived in this country recently and all three had a family of young children. Most of the mothers had either not attended school in this country, or attended only briefly, and had no more than what could be described as 'survival' oral English. Most of the mothers could read and write in their mother tongue, several took newspapers in their mother tongue. Some families had children's books in English, for example from the local library. Where there were older siblings the younger children often had access to their books. Several parents expressed a wish for more children's books from school, which they could have shared with the children; where these were available this was much appreciated.

Development of the children's competence in English was aided by a number of aspects in the home. Where there were older siblings they often helped. Television was a source of enjoyment and of spoken English, also a source of printed English. All the families regarded it as important that the children should experience speaking in and hearing their mother tongue, both to retain their culture and for communicating with relatives in the home, locally and on visits to the Indian subcontinent. Asian videos were borrowed or hired, and these were a frequent weekend experience. In a number of homes stories were told in the mother tongue in which all the children were reported to be fluent. In only one instance was the point made that the child needed to be encouraged to speak the mother tongue. In order to ensure that their children became proficient in their mother tongue and were able to read and write in it these parents tended to send their children to some form of supplementary school from a relatively early age. Some expressed a wish that such tuition could be provided at some stage within school hours.

All the parents regarded education as important for their children's future employment prospects. It is worth noting that only two fathers were not employed and that half of the mothers worked at least part-time. A number of the families had come from villages yet had settled into a town and found employment in an industrial setting. The families all felt welcome in the school, appreciative of what the school was doing, or at least accepting of teachers as the authority knowing best what should be covered. A number of the parents would, however, have appreciated more ongoing contact with the school, and perhaps an opportunity to observe and participate in some activities. For discussions to have been effective would have required an informal atmosphere and someone to translate. For most of the parents their competence in English was adequate for shopping, but not for discussion of schooling. Indeed in a number of the homes the more-able children were acting as interpreters.

Most of the children were thought to have settled relatively quickly into nursery class or reception class. However, it would have helped both children and the parents had they been encouraged to stay with their children initially and given an opportunity to appreciate the purpose of a number of the activities. For the less-able, and those without older brothers and sisters to assist them, it seems particularly important that links with the school be sustained if these children are to make continued progress within the increasingly complex school system.

Nine of the children were in schools where they were among many classmates who spoke the same language. The remaining two children were in a school where they did not have such companions. One of these children had been sent to nursery school to ensure that he would have sufficient competence in English on starting primary school; the other spoke English. Most of the families whose parent was interviewed had currently at least one sibling in the same school; several also had siblings in secondary school. Only two of the families did not have an older sibling in the school, and in both of these families a younger child had already started school. Thus most of the children whose parents we interviewed had a sibling close enough in age to be a playmate; furthermore most parents had some recent experience of that school, of its curriculum and expectations, to compensate for their limited personal experience of education in this country. Their positive feelings about the school were clear from the interviews.

Families of Afro-Caribbean origin

A parent or other relative of nine of the children of Afro-Caribbean origin was interviewed; eight mothers and one grandmother, who after bringing up her own large family was now bringing up several grandchildren. Six girls and three boys were included, and within each sex there was at least one child who had scored high and one low on the language test. All but one of these children was born in this country, that one child had stayed with grandparents in Jamaica until the parents had settled in this country and arrived shortly before entry to reception class. Eight of those interviewed were born in Jamaica and had at least their early education in that country. Most of those interviewed had at least a year or two of secondary education in this country; three had attended or were attending college. Grandparents or another close relative had brought up a number of those interviewed for at least part of their childhood; most had relatives still in Jamaica and several had already returned for a visit. Most of the children had close relatives nearby. However, the families of these young children were very different from those of Asian ethnic origin described earlier. Three of these children were the only child in the home; three others had a younger sibling or cousin in the home; the remaining three had older siblings, but the nearest in age was 13, 16 and 18 respectively. Thus entry to school for the child in this study was for most parents their first contact with that school, even with primary schools in this country.

All these children were attending schools where children of their ethnic background were in a minority, in some instances a very small minority. While they may not have had language problems (such as those experienced by the children of Asian ethnic origin), they did have isolation comparable with the initial experience at school of only children, with the added problem that their parents had been educated in another country. Most of the children had attended nursery school (several had attended a day nursery), and by the time they entered primary school had made friends. One mother reported that she had expected her child to be upset, but it was she herself who was upset, not the child! One of the children who had moved from another area and who had been happy in the day nursery had become increasingly unsettled over time in primary school. She was a child whom we observed to have limited language competence and to be frequently rejected by the other children. Another young child, the only young child in the home (although there were older siblings who had left home), was reported to have been unsettled initially. He found it strange to be with other than his mother and father, and to be with white adults. This child had, however, made impressive progress in reception class, and made a number of close friends. Most of the children were reported to have friends from different ethnic backgrounds.

The children were said to talk about what happened at school, several played schools, often with dolls as children. Most of the mothers reported reading with the child or telling stories, in two instances an older sister also did so. Several children were reported to enjoy reading books either from the school library or which had been bought. A close bond clearly existed between those who were interviewed and their child. Incidents were quoted and the child's out-of-school experiences were graphically described by several interviewees.

Particularly fascinating were the discussions with the relative of the three children who were among the most able in the sample. The first was reported to love asking questions; the child was said to chat too much, and when a reply was not forthcoming on one occasion to have commented: 'Mom, I'm talking to a stone wall!' We had collected numerous examples of this child's rich language in a variety of settings with peers. The second of these able children was reported to have asked lots of questions since an early age and to have even sought on the way to and from day nursery to engage adults in the bus in conversation. Comments on work and progress at school were frequently discussed at home. The child's comment on one occasion was reported to have been: 'I've had a hard day and I haven't had time to play!' This child, although not actually reading when he started school, was now described by his mother as 'a reading addict'. Like the previous child, this child had a selective interest in television, described as mature beyond his years, and a dry sense of humour, which, from the incidents described, his mother shares. The third able child, who was the youngest in a large family, settled easily in school, brought books from the school library, belonged to the local library, and also attempted to read the newspaper and do crosswords. It was reported that books brought from the library are not laid down until they are finished. Interviewing the mothers of these children was reminiscent of the stimulating discussions I had with the parents of the young fluent readers to be discussed in Chapter 11.

The mothers of two of the other children were also interested in their child's progress, felt welcome in school and would visit when necessary. One was working, otherwise she would have visited more often. The remaining four children had some difficulty with the language test. One of these children had been late in learning to speak, but was now making some progress and enjoying school. The mother who was working was unable to visit the school, but the father who was close to the child went instead.

A final question asked of these parents was their views on Creole and patois. It should be noted that all these interviews were of women; the fathers might have expressed different views. Several mothers made a distinction between the way they would speak to Afro-Caribbean friends and relatives, and the way they would speak with the child. In the former situation, some would they said use patois; several did comment that relatives who had brought them up in Jamaica had been strict with them and told them not to speak, as one put it, 'broken English'. There were some Creole features in the spoken language of some of the mothers during the interview, but not such that it made problems for the interviewer.

One mother referring to her own education in Jamaica said: 'It's different what you speak in school and what you write in school is two different things, what you speak is not what you write – it's difficult'. Another mother's response was that she speaks to the child as she spoke in the interview. She also commented proudly that her elder child had English as the best subject at school. Yet another mother commented that her child had said to her: 'You speak Jamaican in the house and you speak English outside.' She did not feel that the child spoke patois much but went on to comment that 'It's part of our heritage', and that the child will pick it up but know when to use it and when not to. Yet another mother commented that she didn't encourage her child to speak patois because she felt it would identify the child as black and 'won't help in life talking like that'. This family had been in England for some time and the mother was born here. She said she tried to avoid prejudice in the house and hoped the child would accept mixing of black and white. A final comment from one of the mothers, who was brought up by her grandparents in Jamaica, was that she was checked, especially for using different letters, for example 'dem' instead of 'them', by her grandmother, who would say: 'Why do you talk like that, you talk as if you just come off the mountains?' Her grandmother said it was broken English and she must not talk like that.

When we studied the transcripts of the children's language in a variety of settings we noticed that there were a number of Creole features. Our Jamaican expert was able to point out to us that some of the features were not, as we might have thought, ungrammatical, but rather they were grammatically different but regular features used to carry meaning.

As we have shown, the parents, all of whom we asked agreed to be interviewed, were very positive in their attitude to school and felt welcome there. Some found it difficult to visit because they were working, however all were willing to take time off for these interviews. During the interviews they showed a warm affection for their children, knowledge of their development and concern that they would be successful and happy.

Families of three indigenous white children

These were all able children, and all three were doing well in school; all read at home and were members of the library. Two of these parents were interested in seeing what was happening in school. The comments of one of these parents, based on her observations in the nursery, are worthy of reporting in detail as they show how much can be gained from encouraging the parents to observe their young children in the preschool and reception class.

> I think the nursery prepared [L] for school . . . she became more relaxed through meeting people . . . I did not expect the nursery to do some things like cooking, nor academic work. I expected more play and singing . . . there was a good continuation into school . . . some of the things the children do in nursery they do again in school but I suppose there has to be repetition . . . I didn't expect the children to do anything towards reading in the nursery, but they did. Perhaps I thought they would learn the alphabet . . . I think a lot of the things they did in the nursery helped to read but I didn't understand it all at the time. I enjoyed helping and think parents should know what their children are doing and why they do it.

COMMENTS

The schools that were selected for this study were what would have been termed 'social priority schools'. They were chosen for their varied proportions of children from different ethnic minority backgrounds and because of different patterns of intake and size of school. In selecting parents for interview we included some whose children's language was advanced, and others who were less-able. However, all the parents we asked to take part made time to talk to us, were enthusiastic about their children's development and positive in their attitude to the school. We found that some parents would have appreciated the opportunity to spend time observing in the school and learning more about the curriculum and the purpose of the various activities. However, the mutual trust which we found between these parents and their children's teachers made us hopeful for these children's future.

Be cautious in making assumptions that any parents are not interested in their children's progress. Where I have contacted parents to discuss their children they have been very willing to do so; I have done this many times, including with parents who the school did not expect to co-operate. Given someone who knows something about the children, is sensitive to their feelings and knowledgeable about education, most parents are very willing to be interviewed at a time convenient to them. Furthermore, they often provide a great deal of insightful information. I hope something of the flavour of these interviews has come through, in spite of the fact that we decided not to present the findings in the form of case studies.

RELATED STUDIES

A related study to that reported in this chapter was conducted by one of my students. She interviewed nursery school head teachers and compared their aims for preschool education with the views of those responsible for the infant department in primary schools without a nursery class. As in the present research, disappointingly little appreciation was shown by the teachers in primary schools concerning the aims of preschool educators (Wallace 1985).

Two dissertations by students in their own preschool units, where most children were from ethnic minorities and had a mother tongue other than English, are relevant to the issue of continuity. Davenport used the observational schedules developed in our researches to study the play of Sikh children in a nursery class and at home (Davenport 1983). Pearson used PLAI to assess the language of children in her nursery school, when they were about to enter the infant department. The children's language was assessed in English and in Punjabi; for the latter testing she was able to call on another of my students whose mother tongue was Punjabi. Selected children were also observed at play and their language recorded in their mother tongue (Pearson 1987). As a consequence of undertaking her study in the nursery school of which she was head teacher, a school where few children had English as their mother tongue, she made changes in the organization of her school. Studies such as these provide important insights for the observer, but also to feed back to staff with regard to choice of activities and organization and for staff development.

As I have shown, this research, which had limited funding from DES, was modified as seemed appropriate to include new aspects not outlined in the initial proposal; we were fortunate that the research committee gave us this flexibility. I was also fortunate that I had a number of students who were enthusiastic to undertake related studies in their own settings.

At the time of this research, and the others described in Chapter 7, few teachers had supportive adults in the reception classroom or other early years classrooms in the primary school for much of the day. In recent years government initiatives, backed by funding, have increased the availability of teaching assistants in primary schools. Consider what roles these additional staff might perform and how their duties might be co-ordinated by the teacher in charge (see Clark 2002 for a discussion of the findings of a government report on their deployment).

CREATING CLASSROOM CULTURES IN THREE SCHOOLS

The emphasis in the researches I have considered so far in this section has been on the need for a supportive environment for young children on transition from one stage of education to another, and for continuity in their educational experiences from preschool to primary and from home to school. A recent study by Gregory and her colleagues of 4-year-olds in three schools considers a related aspect (Gregory et al. 2004). They acknowledge the work of Bernstein, and the views expressed in the 1970s and reported here in chapters 2 and 3, that early school success or failure has long been associated with social class. They point out that recent league tables have confirmed suspicions that children from schools in more affluent areas score generally higher in literacy and numeracy tests. They refer to official reports focusing on deficits and underachievement, and linking this to parents' failure to prepare their children adequately for school. They consider the type of pedagogy in the three very different schools, and what each counted as learning.

This research, which is still ongoing, is a longitudinal study of the home and school literacy experiences of 12 children from age 4 to 7 years in each of the three schools. One of the schools is in a wealthy London suburb; the second in multicultural and multilingual inner London; the third in an economically disadvantaged area in a town on the south coast of England. The data they present in this article is from the children's first or reception year. They make an interesting distinction between the three schools, classifying the classroom in one as a 'haven', the second as 'home from home', the third as a 'tough new world'. They consider what counts as learning in each of the classrooms. One they categorize as learning how to behave; the second, as learning about texts shared with parents; the third as 'trying hard to get it right'! They argue that the types of questions the teachers ask in these very different settings vary, as does what they expect from the children. In one of the schools, 'high expectations were typified by challenging questions on the part of the teacher and the obvious effort made by the children' (Gregory et al. 2004: 103).

The children in one of the schools brought with them the benefits of economic resources from their families; on these the school could build, and if this failed, the home would make good the deficiencies of the school. The children in the other two schools could not have competed with these resources; however, the schools dealt with the deficiencies in very different ways. The researchers claim that in one of these schools the children were still struggling to understand what counted as learning in the classroom as their teacher concerned herself with the children's social behaviour. The teacher in the other school did not expect her children to bring a knowledge of the British language, culture or ways of life with them into school. However, so long as the children 'tried hard' academically they were, for her, doing what counted as learning. It is argued that these children 'though desperately short on resources, were racing ahead with a teacher who respected and shared a similar interpretation of 'work' (trying hard) as the children's families' (Gregory *et al.* 2004: 106).

> Study this article in detail, and watch for the further reports of the research to find out how the children progress with different teachers. Will the gulf between the children from the very different backgrounds increase as the children progress through their primary school, or will one of these approaches give the children a sufficiently positive self-esteem to enable them to succeed against the odds?

What can we learn from children who succeed?

Section IV
What can we learn from
children who discover...?

Chapter 10

Reading and learning to read

INTRODUCTION

I make no apology for the focus in this final section: one of my own researches on children who could read when they entered primary school. This I will contrast for research approach with a community study on children with reading difficulties. Both researches made an international impact when published. My study of young fluent readers (Clark 1976) is still frequently cited, as are a number of my other publications on reading. This is also true of most of the publications to which I will make reference in this chapter (Hall *et al.* 2003; Whitehead 2004). As with many of my researches, the first, a community study of 1544 children, was made possible by enlisting the help of students, who undertook some of the individual testing. The aims of the two researches were very different, for that reason so too were the approach and the sample; the first was large scale, the second intensive. They therefore make valuable illustrative material to bring educational research alive.

CASE STUDIES

The young fluent readers in my study, and those in a more recent research by Stainthorp and Hughes (1999; 2004), although they were studied over a period of years, were only identified after they could read.

> Thus the information on the years before they entered school was 'retrospective' and depended on the parents' memory of events. It is difficult to obtain large samples of 'normal' preschool children and, particularly, to study these intensively, yet unobtrusively, during their early years. Perhaps it is for this reason that a number of classical studies in linguistics are of the linguists' own children. You may find some interesting case studies, or you could make a study of an individual child yourself.

The following four case studies of a single child are fascinating, and are of interest in relation to learning to read:

- Butler (1975), one of Marie Clay's students in New Zealand, made a detailed study of her multiply handicapped granddaughter Cushla and her early interactions with books.
- Bissex (1980), a student of Courtney Cazden in the United States, recorded her son Paul's earliest attempts at writing, both before he started school and during his early years in school.
- Payton (1984), one of my students, recorded her daughter Cecilia's conversations about print and related these to her attempts at written communication before she could read or had started school.
- Van Lierop (1985), another of my students, was able to make use for her dissertation of diary notes that she had made previously of her young daughter's earliest experiences of print.

The availability of sophisticated recording devices has made it possible to obtain recordings of the language of young children in their homes without the intrusion of an observer (by using radio microphones), although an observer is still important to identify the context in which the interactions took place (see chapters 3 and 5).

> There is a greater appreciation now of the importance of the foundations of literacy many children acquire before the actual teaching of reading commences than at the time I conducted my research. Would you agree that there are still those in education who ignore the evidence on the extent to which the foundations of literacy are laid for many children before school, and the contribution of the home, both preschool and out of school?

CHANGING PERSPECTIVES ON READING

For many years, parents, and also staff in preschool units, were discouraged from beginning to teach children to read before their entry to primary school. Gradually the emphasis has changed. Not only do primary schools introduce children to reading soon after they enter the school, but preschool units are also encouraged to introduce aspects of print to their young children. In recent years (until 2004) in England, not only would children of 7 years of age have been assessed on Standard Assessment Tasks (SATs) at the end of Key Stage 1, but league tables would also have been prepared showing the ranking of the children and the schools. Yet in many countries children do not learn to read until about 7 years of age; indeed they may not start school until then. The government in England now has a powerful role, not only in determining on what the children will be tested and when, but also how reading will be taught and how much of the school day will be devoted to literacy and numeracy.

This book is not the place to make a detailed analysis of changing views on the development of literacy. There is a greater appreciation now of the contribution of the home, at the preschool stage and beyond, to children's development of literacy in our modern print-filled environment, also of the out-of-school environment generally. *New Directions in the Study of Reading* contains reprints of some key publications and brief reports of more recently completed researches (Clark 1985b). Two chapters may be of particular interest to readers who are students as they were written by students of mine (who had been encouraged to prepare articles for publication). One is a study of concepts of print in children attending her nursery school (Sutton 1985); the other the case study by Van Lierop mentioned above.

A second valuable reference is *Awakening to Literacy* (Goelman, Oberg and Smith 1984), which contains papers by 14 internationally respected researchers with extensive and overlapping backgrounds in education, psychology, sociology, anthropology and linguistics, whose professional experience covers many parts of the world, from areas where literacy is assumed to others where literacy is limited, even in the adult population. Two chapters are of particular interest, those of Ferreiro (1984), who studied the initial attempts of Spanish-speaking children to make sense of written language, and of Donaldson (1984), who analysed the relationship of learning speech to learning about writing. In *Young Literacy Learners: how we can help them* (Clark 1994) there are more recent references and insights from practical work that I undertook in a primary school in Birmingham; also considered are the return to an emphasis on phonics in the early teaching of reading (phonics with a purpose), the relationship between spoken and written language and the developing awareness of print in preschool children.

The House of Commons Education and Skills Committee announced an enquiry into The Teaching of Reading in November 2004. It is clear from the evidence submitted that the place of phonics is still a highly controversial area (see the oral evidence from 8 December 2004 and 7 February 2005). The report was published in April 2005.

THE SETTING FOR THE RESEARCHES

In the 1960s and 1970s, when I undertook the two researches that I will discuss in the following chapter, the emphasis was very different from that of today. It is worth reminding readers just how different the views were.

> If you look at textbooks on reading published in the 1960s you will find that the teaching of reading was considered a skill to be taught, and learnt almost exclusively in the first few years in school, thereafter practised, extended and

developed into silent reading for comprehension. Thus only teachers who would teach either children in their first two years in school, or older backward readers, were likely to have had lectures on the teaching of reading during their training.

Teachers working in preschool units would have been strongly discouraged from introducing the beginnings of reading or writing to the children in their care. This may seem ironic now, when children of the same age, say at 4 years of age, may in many local authorities in England already be in 'reception class'. Parents and teachers of preschool children were expected to send the children into the primary school 'ready' to learn to read; beyond that would have been regarded as inappropriate interference by parents with the work of the primary school, even by preschool teachers.

Much of the research in the 1960s concentrated on the relative merits of different methods for the initial teaching of reading, on the characteristics of backward readers or on trends in reading standards. The pervasiveness of this view was illustrated by the response I got when I sought children who entered school already reading with understanding for the research I was about to undertake.

Many teachers believed I was unlikely to find children already reading on entry to school, at least in their school! Parents whose children were already reading with understanding on entry to school were embarrassed; some had been made to feel guilty, both by neighbours and by some of the teachers whose schools the children entered. Whether parents' attitudes to education were positive and supportive tended to be measured in terms of the frequency of their visits to school in an appropriately enquiring and accepting frame of mind, numbers of books in the home or social class. To what extent do you think this is still true in schools you know?

In the 1960s, assessment of children's readiness for reading and the respective strengths and weaknesses of good and backward readers were normally measured by standardized 'psychometric' tests. Intelligence tests would have been used to assess the child's general level of functioning. On the basis of that, some prediction of the child's expected progress in learning to read might be made, failure explained and even a profile of backward readers' strengths and weaknesses drawn-up. Various tests of visual and auditory discrimination and motor co-ordination were applied in reading readiness tests and in diagnoses of the problems of backward readers. Reading progress would be measured in young children by individual tests in which the child read aloud a series of isolated words of increasing difficulty; a reading age was assessed from the accuracy of the child's oral reading Alternatively a test that contained sentences or paragraphs of increasing difficulty might be read aloud by the child; a reading age for accuracy, comprehension and speed would be assessed on the basis of the accuracy of the child's oral reading. Comprehension tests of silent reading might be group tests with multiple-choice answers. More sophisticated measures are now available, and we have greater appreciation of the effect of the purpose, the text and the context, and of the influence of silent and oral reading, on children's reading performance. Nonetheless, revised versions of a number of the tests common in the 1960s are still used in the classroom!

> What measures are now used to assess the reading accuracy and comprehension of young children?

Three important developments of relevance to learning to read occurred in the 1970s. In 1971 the first edition of Frank Smith's book *Understanding Reading* (Smith 1971), initially regarded as revolutionary in outlook and later as highly controversial in its stance, was published in the United States, to be followed by a number of other texts in the following years. In 1972 a Committee of Enquiry into the teaching of reading in schools in England was set up under the chairmanship of Sir Alan Bullock (*A Language for Life*, DES 1975a) (the Bullock Report). Also in 1972 Marie Clay's book *Reading: the patterning of complex behaviour* was first published, in New Zealand (Clay 1972). This was followed in 1991 by an updated book entitled *Becoming Literate* (Clay 1991).

In the Bullock Report the need for a whole-school policy towards the teaching of reading in primary and secondary schools was emphasized (DES 1975a). Smith noted the importance of considering what the adult reader does, and what the beginner reader is trying to do in processing text; he stressed the need to appreciate the complexity of the skills a young child brings to the task of reading for which so little credit was given (Smith 1971). Clay studied the type and range of errors made not just by those who were having difficulty in learning to read, but also by young children who were making progress in the early stages of learning to read (Clay 1972). The test of Concepts of Print, the Reading Recovery programme, for children with difficulties, and the use of running records to assess children's reading are all based on the work of Marie Clay (Clay 1991).

> Both Clay and Smith stressed the importance of considering reading as a complex process of understanding language through a written medium, not primarily as a visual skill. What implications does this view have for the teaching of reading and writing?

WHY STUDY YOUNG FLUENT READERS?

My interest in children who were already reading when they started school was aroused by two incidents. First, I attended a lecture on reading, during which the speaker commented that in reading, and in education generally, most research tended to analyse failures, whereas in many areas of skill the aim was to learn from studying those who were successful and their attributes. Shortly after this, a teacher contacted me to discuss a boy who entered her infant department at 5 years of age already reading fluently; this was the first time that this experienced teacher had encountered such a child. I visited the school and became interested in the child, whose progress I followed over the years. He was the first child I had met who was reading fluently when he started school. Not only could he read with ease, he could spell and was fascinated by numbers and letters and the different types of print in which these could be represented. He was also a wonderful mimic, which got him into trouble on one occasion as he acted out the head teacher taking school assembly! This boy was not from a professional home. His infant teacher, who had contacted me, supported and encouraged him throughout his education. These two incidents made me decide it was important to learn from children such as these.

Chapter II

Young fluent readers and children with difficulties

Two contrasting research approaches

BACKGROUND

In this chapter I will contrast the approach in my research into children who were already reading with fluency, understanding and enjoyment when they started school at 5 years of age with an earlier research, a longitudinal community study of children with reading difficulties. The focus will be on what we can learn from children who succeed. My aim in comparing these two studies is to illustrate the importance of choosing a plan for research to fit the aims. So often students appear to believe that the larger the sample, the better the research. Finally, I will compare my research on young fluent readers with a more recent study, which the authors claim was inspired by my research.

> Any research, no matter how well it is funded, will have to meet a deadline; planning decisions at the onset will have consequences for the detail in which any aspect can be investigated. You have to decide whether it is important to study a limited number of children or schools in depth, or a large sample more superficially. On occasion researchers may choose to follow a superficial initial study with in-depth research into a selected sub-sample. If you decide to undertake a longitudinal research, this has disadvantages as well as advantages. There is the real danger of sample loss, and this loss will not be random.

I will use a comparison of the two researches to show why and in what ways the approach in the two studies was so different and the limitations each approach gave to the generalizability of the findings. When reporting the first research, the community study of reading difficulties, I will explain at each step why I made the choices I did, and hopefully provide you with a framework for comparing other more recent studies, and for planning your own. With the second study I will take a different approach, initially only giving a summary of the findings. Hopefully this will raise questions to which you would expect answers; I will then answer some of the questions that I would have expected.

READING DIFFICULTIES IN SCHOOLS

Background to the study

The aim of the research was to investigate the incidence of severe and continuing reading difficulties in a normal school population, in particular among children of average intelligence. The term 'dyslexia' for such children was used by some professionals but not by others. Controversy surrounded the use of the term, the incidence of children with such reading disability, whether there were clearly defined characteristics and whether therefore a particular remedial approach was required. Since most of the available information was based on highly selected clinic cases, the SED agreed to fund my research to provide data on both the incidence of such disabilities and the associated characteristics. One aim was to enable the SED to respond to those who claimed that there was insufficient provision for such children, who it was claimed needed highly specialized methods. Throughout the research I used the neutral term 'severe reading difficulties', rather than what was at the time an emotive term, 'dyslexia'.

Because of the aims of this research all children of a given age group who entered primary school in one local authority formed the initial sample; the reading level of each of these 1544 children was individually assessed when they were about 7 years of age. This large sample also made it possible to secure community incidence figures for 7-year-olds for a number of features which some had suggested were directly associated with severe reading difficulties. The second phase of the study included all the children with low scores on the initial reading test, whose reading was again tested individually, as was their spelling and intelligence. The final phase included all of those children a year later who had low scores on the reading test at the second stage and who were shown to be of average intelligence.

The sample

The research took place in Dunbartonshire, a highly industrialized part of Scotland, with a number of small schools in outlying areas. The primary school population there at the time was about one-twentieth that of Scotland as a whole; there were 66 schools with primary school pupils and three special schools. All were in the initial sample, and furthermore all schools co-operated throughout the research.

It was important to choose children with an equal length of time in school. As in many areas, some schools had only one entry date, others more than one. For that reason the sample was chosen by date of birth. It was found that a birth date from 1 April to 31 August would ensure that all children had by the time of testing been in school for a similar length of time. The study commenced when these children were around 7 years of age and had been in school about

2 years; this was felt to be the earliest it was appropriate to screen for backwardness in reading.

All appropriate children at each stage in this research were included. Many moved school within the county, these were followed; only those who left the county were lost to the study (2.7 per cent).

> I hope you appreciate the importance in this research of choosing a sample matched for time spent in school. It is important to ensure that all absentees are included, even though this may be very time consuming. When you read reports of large-scale studies, check whether you are provided with sufficient data to assess the reliability of the findings. Do the researchers indicate how many of the chosen schools, or children, failed to take part, and what action was taken to compensate for that? Particularly where group testing is employed, consider what action was taken to include absentees; is the number missing even stated? Where, as here, the research is longitudinal, what proportion of the sample remained throughout?

It is not possible to give the full details in this brief summary; however, in the published version of this research all the above information was provided (Clark 1970, and a second edition in 1979).

The research design

There were three stages to the research, from the large-scale community test initially when the children were about 7 years of age, to all backward readers at 8 years of age, and to a smaller sample followed up until they were 9 years of age. All the testing was individual, and was made possible with the help of volunteers; undergraduate psychology students and students training as teachers who were trained to undertake the initial testing. As you will appreciate, individual testing of the majority of the age group in a school was not the greatest problem; what was time consuming was 'catching' those who were frequently absent and following those who moved school.

Stage I

The sample was 1544 children (791 boys and 753 girls) who were tested on a simple oral reading test of individual words, also a vocabulary test, laterality tests (of handedness, footedness and eyedness), left–right differentiation and motor co-ordination. This provided useful community incidence figures for aspects of development some people, using limited clinic samples, had claimed to be associated with specific reading difficulty. Information was also collected on absence and changes of school during the children's first two years in primary school. The initial testing took about half an hour per child.

Stage 2

This involved 230 children (138 boys and 92 girls) from the initial sample, all those who had been shown not to have developed any independent reading skill as assessed when they were 7 years of age. In addition to a further individual reading test these children's spelling was tested and their intelligence was assessed by an educational psychologist. A questionnaire about the children's adjustment was completed by the teachers. Information on attendance and changes of school during the third year was collected. The testing of each child took approximately 2 hours.

Stage 3

Children who were still backward readers and of average intelligence were studied in more detail. These children were assessed on a wide range of tests by qualified educational psychologists, including further reading tests for accuracy and comprehension and diagnostic reading tests, language tests and tests of auditory and visual discrimination and motor co-ordination; their attitude to reading was also assessed. The double criteria of continued low reading combined with average intelligence had been met by 70 children (47 boys and 23 girls), only one of these, one boy, had left the county by the third stage. This was the experimental group to whom the extended battery of tests was administered, which took about half a day per child. A second group was included, although not for the lengthy language test; this group was comparable for intelligence, but had less severe reading difficulty. Parents of 111 children (69 experimental and 42 control) still in the study at this stage were contacted to seek their permission for hearing and vision testing, which was undertaken in local clinics. Details were collected from head teachers as to what remedial help these children had received in school. The results of the 19 most severely backward children were considered in some detail; when these children were 10 years of age a parent of each was interviewed.

> The emphasis so far has been on the plan of this research. I hope you appreciate the reasons for the steps taken at each stage of this research. Before turning to the contrasting study I will give you a brief outline of some of the key findings.

Brief outline of the results

From an initial sample of 1544 children only a few children of average intelligence were found to have severe and prolonged difficulty in learning to read. Furthermore, there was no single group of symptoms that distinguished these children; thus it did not appear that one particular specialized method would have been appropriate to help such children. The majority of these children were boys (15 boys and 4 girls). Most of these children had intelligence in the low average category. Speech defects were common, as was poor visuo-motor co-ordination. There was little evidence of active participation on the part of the parents, though the parents were positive in their attitude to the school. Most of the children came from large families, and their reading material seemed to be mainly that supplied by the school. In general, the difficulties of these children were not specific to the problem of deciphering words on a printed page; they appeared to need assistance on a wide range of activities.

The striking finding, therefore, was the small number of such children and the diversity of their disabilities, with no underlying pattern common to the group. The approach adopted and the size of sample made certain that the final results would stand up to scrutiny, and that a number of generalizations could be made which were important for policy and practice.

> Do not take this as evidence that there are *no* children of high intelligence who have severe and prolonged difficulties with reading and writing. During my career I have met a number of such children and adults. What was found, however, was that even in a sample as large as this, with large classes and limited provision for remedial help, no such children were found. The cautions outlined above should convince you that it is unlikely that any children of that age in that area, at that time, were missed by this research.

Valuable information on community incidence figures was obtained during the course of this research. We became aware of a number of important points, including the poor attendance record of many of the backward readers and the number of changes of school encountered by many young children during their early years in primary school. We were also able to show that there was no association between a number of features and backwardness in reading, including left-handedness and crossed laterality. We found that crossed laterality (different preferred hand and eye), which was being claimed to be associated with reading difficulty, was much higher in the normal population than was usually appreciated Around 39 per cent of children had different preferred hand and eye. Inability to differentiate right and left was found to be much more common than was appreciated, even when the children were 7 years of age. Another interesting finding, from the spelling test when the children were 8 years of age, was that reversals of letters and words were very common in backward readers; the poorer their reading the more such reversals were found. Our large initial sample enabled us to provide incidence figures for left-handedness, showing that at that time nearly 9 per cent used their left hand for writing, but with a greater incidence in boys than girls (boys 10.9 per cent and girls 6.5 per cent). The figures for those writing with their left hand have increased a great deal since that time; however, a sex difference remains. More boys than girls are backward in reading and the more prolonged and severe the difficulty the greater the proportion of boys. The above findings illustrate the error in placing undue emphasis on any of these features in cases of young backward readers found in clinic as if they were very unusual, something I had found common in the records to which I had access.

> I hope this makes you realize how important it is to check for community incidence figures before drawing conclusions from clinic cases. In any research you study do check whether information is provided on the numbers of boys and girls in the sample. Such information is not always provided, yet in many aspects of attainment there are sex differences.

Limitations in the research

It should be appreciated that no matter how large a sample, there are limitations to the justified conclusions from a research; the design adopted is a further defining factor. It must be stressed that from a research planned in the way described above no *causal* relationships between the children's characteristics and backwardness in reading should be deduced.

> This is perhaps a difficult concept to grasp. Nonetheless it is crucial that you appreciate it; you may find a tendency to draw conclusions in some researches about causal relationships where that is not legitimate. The fact that two things are seen to be present at the same time does not mean that one caused the other. Even if it did, there is no way of telling from such evidence which thing caused the other.

The following will perhaps illustrate this point. Beyond a certain age you will have less calcium in your bones and fewer aunts still living. These facts do not mean that your lack of calcium caused your aunts to die, or that their death was related to changes in your bone structure; the missing variable there is, of course, age!

Likewise young children who are backward in reading may be found to be troublesome, or may have certain weaknesses in their perceptual abilities or limitations in their vocabulary. If one wishes to understand the causal relationships between any of these features and progress in reading, then it is essential to undertake *not a larger study, but one with a different design*; one in which the children's behaviour, perceptual abilities or vocabulary, for example, have been assessed *before* their backwardness in reading has been identified. There are serious dangers when assumptions are made about a relationship between certain features of a child's development or background and progress in reading. At the time of this research parents and teachers were inclined to anticipate difficulties in learning to read if certain features were found, not least left-handedness.

To investigate causal relationships in the development of reading it is important to undertake a longitudinal research in which the children are studied from before they are found to have difficulties in reading, indeed even from before the instruction in reading commences. This is true of other aspects of development also, for example behavioural difficulties or speech difficulties. Bear these points in mind when evaluating research and take care in any claims you make for causal relationships in your own researches.

YOUNG FLUENT READERS

Background to the study

Unlike the previous study this research began as the children entered primary school, children who were already reading on entry. My plan was to include a number of tests similar to those used with backward readers. Clearly these children were, in some ways, advanced well beyond their years. I wondered whether there were any weaknesses *in spite of which* they had achieved such progress, possibly even some that were being used to explain failure to learn to read in other children?

A second reason for choosing such children was that I might find evidence to challenge some assumptions about essential ingredients in reading instruction in school. If children are expected to learn to read in a group situation, in a classroom and at a given age, some of these features may place a child in a vulnerable position just because of the group situation or the expectations of the teachers. It is dangerous, however, to go further and assume that all these features are necessary ingredients without which one cannot learn to read in any situation. As I noted earlier the fact that certain factors are found to be associated with lack of progress does not entitle one to assume they are the cause of the failure. Some factors, even if causally related to lack of progress, may be so only within certain approaches to learning to read. Finally, there may be some factors which influence the learning if it takes place in a group situation, such as a classroom.

Thus, my community study of reading difficulties provided a framework from which this further study was planned. It seemed important to study children's approach to learning to read in detail, from as early as possible, and to explore the home background within which this had taken place. When I undertook this research, few children attended preschool education, making it difficult to identify a wide enough sample of such children earlier than their entry to primary school. I appreciated that children who were already competent readers on entry to school were indeed very precocious, yet I hoped that a study of their strengths and weaknesses would provide insights of relevance to the teaching of young children and also aid our understanding of ways to help backward readers.

How would you have selected children for this study, and what aspects of their development would you have studied?

A summary of the research unfortunately reveals little of the richness of the qualitative information; for that you would have to seek out a copy of the book *Young Fluent Readers* (Clark 1976), which although a research report is brought alive with numerous quotations from the children and their parents and teachers (see also Clark 1984 for a further analysis of some of the data). It became clear during the research how stimulating and how much of a challenge these children would be to any teacher who found them in her class. It also revealed how much the context in which they were expected to operate influenced the competence and creativity they were able to exhibit. Clearly the classroom provided stimulation for some; for others it was limiting rather than challenging. Some were shown to be capable of a variety of complex achievements, which the diet provided in the classroom never allowed them to reveal. These included a wide range of reading, the ability to compose interesting stories, breadth of knowledge, ability to work out complex calculations involving large numbers, some appreciation of the layout of a map, the ability to play chess (even at an early age) – and not least, a sense of fun.

These children's comprehension of print at an early age is perhaps best captured by the two following examples, rather than by their impressive scores on a reading test on entry to school. One child was reported by a parent to have read a poster in a bus stating 'Friday night is danger night'. His response had been 'It's a good job it's Saturday'. A second child, on entry to school at under 5 years of age, was said by his mother, with some diffidence, to be reading. The teacher reported that she handed him a letter intended for his mother to see what, if any, words he could recognize. In the letter, the teacher had mentioned the 7-year period over which they would have contact. This boy remarked in a tone of utmost concern: 'Whew! Seven whole years!'

A comment from one of the children when 6 years of age seems to sum up the attitude of the group to school: although he enjoyed school he wondered whether it was worth all the time it took up! To quote: 'Well I'm rather surprised when I come home from school to see the time it's taken up. Six whole hours – or five and three-quarters. I do like school but I don't like the time it takes up.'

One boy didn't like reading in school because the books were 'awful boring'. Another child's answer to the same question was that he didn't like certain kinds of sums. When asked why he replied 'They are too easy.' To redress the balance, however, one young child in making a realistic assessment of himself commented: 'Well one thing is certain, I don't like hard work!'

The summary for the study of young fluent readers given here is comparable to that at the end of the full research report (Clark 1976: ch. 9). I will now provide brief answers to some of the questions I hope will have occurred to the reader.

Consider what information you would now expect to be provided about the sample from which these examples were drawn.

Summary

Sample

Thirty-two children (20 boys and 12 girls) from 25 schools, referred shortly after commencing school as already reading fluently, were observed over a period of years. Their initial and later attainment and other characteristics were studied together with their early experiences and home background.

Attainment

When first seen the children's reading attainment was already beyond that which defines children as 'at risk'. The range of reading attainment was from 7 years 6 months to over 11 years of age on an oral reading test. All read with understanding a variety of reading material as well as books – many reading non-fiction as well as fiction. Most were already able to spell at least simple regular words; they also knew when they were wrong and their errors were usually a good approximation to English. Their handwriting was, however, not necessarily even of a standard expected of a child of their age. Most were well above average in arithmetic – especially when the tasks were presented orally in problem form. Their attainment was therefore not limited to the reading situation; on the contrary, most showed skills in a variety of language-based situations.

Intelligence and other characteristics

As a group the children were above average in intelligence, and some were outstandingly gifted. Some, however, were of average intelligence as measured by the tests. Their strengths tended to be in the verbal rather than non-verbal aspects of the tests. The issue was raised as to the extent to which their high level of functioning owed anything to the stimulating language environment in which they were developing. It was felt that it would be wrong to dismiss them as merely a group of unusually intelligent children and to attribute their precocious reading development solely to an innate potential.

Although the group scored high on a test of auditory discrimination a caution was sounded that their success might owe much to the language context of the task. It was also suggested that the failures of other children might well stem from lack of such language skills rather than a weakness in auditory discrimination, even of speech sounds. On visual discrimination, on the contrary, few of these children were above average; a finding which was felt to have implications for remediation of children with reading difficulties.

Furthermore some of these children did not have particularly good motor co-ordination.

Early experiences and home background

The children came from a variety of home backgrounds; some were from large families, others 'only' children and several had been adopted. Some parents had higher education and were in the professions; others had left school early and had no further training. All parents did, however, seem to value education and to wish for their children what they had themselves experienced – or what they had missed. The mothers and those fathers who were interviewed clearly found their families both stimulating and absorbing. Most of the fluent readers had available at some time pre school an interested adult who talked to and listened to them. Few mothers were working at the time of the first interview and those who were by the time of the later interview tended to have selected occupations and hours that enabled them to be available to their families as much as possible. The children were encouraged towards choice of reading material by their mothers, most of whom read widely, and they were also selective in their television viewing.

The parents found it difficult to differentiate the development of their children who were early fluent readers from the other members of the family, most of whom were also successful in school. The commonest characteristics to be mentioned were concentration and self-sufficiency; this meant the children could enjoy the company of others, yet in its absence be content on their own. They were felt to have a high sensitivity to new or unusual experiences.

Few of the parents had consciously attempted to teach their children to read and indeed some were embarrassed at their children's early rapid progress. An interest in their children's progress was coupled with encouragement of independence of choice and of their children's views in any discussions. Borrowing from the local library was an extensive source of reading material; encouraged by parents initially, later sustained by the children themselves. A number of the children had available to them an interested adult with time to devote to them at the stage when they were interested in learning to read – either to read to them, talk with them or answer their questions. Most of the children appeared to have read silently either from the beginning or from an early stage; this made it difficult for parents to pinpoint exactly when they began to read. For some of the children their initial interest was in environmental print at least as much as in books, including captions in the world around, information in the daily papers and on television.

School progress and later development

Reports from school indicated that these fluent readers continued to show impressive attainment in reading, spelling and in written work. Examples of written work were sent by some teachers as an indication of its quality. The children also appeared well-adjusted to school and to be seen as generally acceptable to their classmates; some were indeed popular leaders.

Diaries kept by the children indicated their range of reading. Their other interests at the time of the school reports were studied in a further interview. The extent to which the local library was a regular and valuable resource for most was apparent, as was the children's breadth of interest, and not least the sense of fun of a number of them, coupled with the complexity of the language they used to express this.

QUESTIONS AND ANSWERS

Any professional consulting a summary of a research that has implications for education written by the researcher or by, for example, a reviewer or journalist will naturally be reading to grasp the main essentials and implications.

> You should be alert to the questions to which answers should be available in the more detailed presentation. If no such source is cited, even more caution should be exercised in acceptance of findings. With regard to this research, first list some of your queries and then read the following section, where hopefully I have answered some of them.

As you may have noted this study was of 32 children from 25 schools, with unequal numbers of boys and girls. This should immediately have raised a number of questions about the way the sample was selected. A letter was sent around a large number of schools, and from the responses from the schools 32 children were found to meet the predefined criterion of reading, which was that when tested they could read at least 25 words on a graded word reading test (the same one that was used in the community study). The aim was to study children who entered school already able to read sufficiently well to be beyond the risk of failure found in many of those studied earlier. We rejected any child referred who could only read the occasional word or recognize some letters. Clearly from the information given above, some schools had more than one child in the sample. More of those who were referred and were sufficiently advanced to be included in the study were boys. This is interesting in view of the excess of boys in studies of children with difficulties in reading.

Therefore the sample was not selected in such a way as to have either equal numbers from each school or equal numbers of boys and girls; that might be an important feature of the design for some studies. In the schools that were contacted there may have been many more children such as these, who for a variety of reasons were either not recognized by the schools or referred for the research. From this study it is thus not possible to estimate how common it is for children to enter school already reading with fluency and understanding.

A very different design, including 'screening' of all children individually on entry to school, or approaching schools with carefully chosen different characteristics, would have been necessary. In planning a research it is important to weigh up the costs in time and resources of different approaches, and to relate these to the aims of the study.

> Since most children now attend some form of preschool it would now be possible to identify young fluent readers at a much earlier age. You might find it interesting to undertake a case study of some of these children and their families, including some of the ideas mentioned above.

I have mentioned in a number of places throughout this book the dangers of generalizing from incomplete samples because those lost are not likely to be a 'cross section' of the original sample. In this research I had a high level of continued co-operation. My decision not to continue to follow these children for any longer was made partly because it was realized that the loss to the sample would have increased. An important reason was my growing awareness that to continue to single out these children from their classmates and brothers and sisters might well have adverse effects on their development, or their family relationships. I had promised to keep the information on the children and their families from the press. In spite of my care, information was 'leaked' to the press by one of the families in a school where there was a second child in the study. I managed to persuade the press to divulge no more about the study; however, that finally caused me to stop the research for fear of further revelations.

The children's reading was assessed on tests and on books. The number of children scoring at each level on the tests was noted, and whether there appeared to be any differences in the reading scores or interests related to the children's intelligence or their sex. I was fully aware of the dangers when using a small sample of quoting any results as percentages.

> Be suspicious where you find percentages quoted from very small samples. Check whether the percentage in question might have been derived from only one child! I still see elaborate computerized presentations, perhaps of tables, in percentages. I attend conferences and referee journal articles and am horrified at how often this still occurs; in some instances the sample size is not even mentioned beside the table.

Information is given in the book on the children's spelling scores and the type of errors they made, also whether or not they were able to complete the tests. The children's attempts at spelling were analysed further some time later to see the extent to which they used lower case and capital letters for complete words or parts of words, with some very interesting results (see Clark 1984).

Several intelligence tests were given to the children, on the results of which quantitative and qualitative information is provided. The choice of tests was influenced by the aim to provide 'profiles' of the strengths and weaknesses of these children for comparison with those of older backward readers. In most studies of children who present severe and prolonged difficulties in reading, an excess of boys over girls has been found. It was thus interesting to find an excess of boys in this study, and necessary also to compare test scores for the sexes separately.

Much of the information about the children's early development was gained from parental interviews, and information on their later development in school from a school report. Most of the interview material was taped and then transcribed. This made it possible to have someone less involved in the actual interview 'search' the transcripts for comparable information, allowing the interviewer to conduct the interviews with the children and their parents in as natural a way as possible.

> You will find the full range of items covered in the first parental interview listed at the end of this book (Appendix 3). This may prove helpful if you wish to plan a parental interview, whether concerning children who had success early or children reported to have had reading difficulties. Consider what further questions you would now wish to include. You would certainly want information on availability and use of computers.

As I have stressed, we were interested not only in the children's strengths, but also in any weaknesses, birth difficulties, delays in development or family problems in spite of which these children were so successful so early. This is why the parental interview included questions on a full range of developmental and other features normally asked in clinics concerning children who have failed in learning to read. The importance of this aspect of the study can perhaps best be shown by the following information concerning handedness.

There were in this group of young fluent readers three left-handed children, and three of mixed handedness (associated by some with failed readers only). All six children were highly intelligent. One of the boys of mixed handedness read when tested initially at 5 years of age on the level of an 11-year-old, and could already read the daily paper with understanding on starting school. His spelling was also on the level of a 10-year-old. His mother reported high blood pressure during pregnancy and frequent miscarriages, and that the child suffered from concussion at an early age. Needless to say these are not being recommended as a way to achieve a precocious child! Had this child, however, shown delay in learning to read, there might at that time have been danger of this being attributed to one or other of the above features.

> This, I hope, illustrates for you the importance of care in assessing whether or not there is a causal link between various features in a child's development.

> Be aware of the danger of anticipating inevitable failure in a child who exhibits some of the characteristics that are often said to be found in backward children.

The abilities of the children were widely varied and not confined to the reading situation, although not all scored high on a conventional intelligence test. Few of the children had received formal instruction in reading; however, the support and involvement of adults, usually parents, in dynamic oral interactions with the children in a variety of settings was impressive. The strengths of these children appeared to be in a growing sensitivity to spoken and written language rather than a high level of visuo–motor development.

All the children in the study entered school with two things in common: the ability and the desire to read at an early age. There were few other ways in which they were similar. The interests of the young fluent readers covered many aspects of print, and not only stories. The print in their environment, non-fiction, reference books and daily newspapers were all of interest. Teachers, and parents, do not always appreciate the potential of this wide range of printed material as a resource from which young children can learn to appreciate the functions and features of written communication. Currently the same is probably true for computers, videos and DVDs, with which so many children are already familiar before they start school.

These young fluent readers were interacting with written language; they were, furthermore, becoming successful not only in extracting meaning from print, but also in predicting the likely sequences of letters in words in the English language, leading to high progress in learning to spell. They were also becoming aware of the characteristics of written language as a form of communication that they could use effectively themselves. It is all too easy to say they are rare or atypical or intelligent or from good homes, and to claim that while their development is interesting it has no relevance for the busy teacher faced with a child of average or below average intelligence, from a poor home thought to show little interest and supply little encouragement.

> What are the implications of this research for classroom teachers? The fact that there are children who learn to read without formal instruction, the use of simplified or vocabulary-controlled texts or a stage of oral reading preceding silent reading for understanding does not necessarily mean that all children, left to their own devices, would learn to read. The attributes of the particular child are important and we must not underestimate the crucial role of the environment. Remember that it was only when the settings were sufficiently creative that even children such as these were able to show the extent of their abilities and knowledge. Any theory of reading is adequate only in so far as it takes account of such children.

While these children learnt to read early, it is pertinent that many of their siblings learnt quickly and effortlessly shortly after entry to school. There was not a plentiful supply of books in the homes of all these young children. Libraries played an important role in catering for and in stimulating the interests of these children. For most of the children the stimulus to use the library came initially from the parents, though the children themselves soon found it a valuable source of information and enjoyment. The findings have implications for libraries and schools with regard to the accessibility of different types of reading material, layout, advice and flexibility of regulations to ensure that children without continuing support of a kind available to these children also have access to reading material to suit their developing interests.

> You might finding it interesting to undertake a study in a primary school or preschool unit to check how wide a range of reading material, fiction and non-fiction, is accessible to young children, and whether, where appropriate, there are books in a variety of languages. Check also the borrowing arrangements for the children, and whether they can take books home to share with family. You may find a tendency to stay too closely within an age-related structure in considering children's likely interests. There is still reluctance in some schools to allow some of the children to take books home. Armed with this information you could explore with the teachers their reasons for the choices and arrangements. Interviews with the young children would provide valuable insights on their perceptions about the comparable reading environments of home and school.

Many of the children who appear to value the local library and use it extensively come from homes such as those described in this present study. It is important to consider ways in which the local library and the school library can attract young readers who are less fortunate than the families in this study, and sustain their interest. Developments have been made over recent years to encourage parents to share books, even with their babies, to talk to their young children about books and, most importantly, appreciate the contribution they can make to their children's development.

YOUNG EARLY READERS AND NON-EARLY READERS

In recent years the Government, in England in particular, has taken an increasingly powerful role in determining on what and when children, even young children, will be tested, and also how reading will be taught and how much of the school day will be devoted to literacy and numeracy.

In the final part of this chapter I will discuss briefly a research that the authors claim was inspired by my 'groundbreaking work'. My research on young children who were reading with fluency and understanding when they started school began in 1969. Twenty-four years later, Rhona Stainthorp and Diana Hughes found that no one had attempted to replicate my study. With the existence of the National Curriculum (in England) and SATs, they decided to undertake a similar study, following their sample through Key Stage 1 and the children's assessment on SATs. Since then they have followed these children through Key Stage 2, until the end of primary school at 11 years of age.

Stainthorp and Hughes undertook case studies of 15 children whom they identified as already functioning at least on the level expected of children at the end of Key Stage 1 (at 7 years of age). The research is reported in *Learning from Children who Read at an Early Age* (Stainthorp and Hughes 1999); they have also published a number of related articles. Through an advertisement in preschool settings they appealed for children who were not yet 5 years old and but were already able to read. They were contacted by parents with whom they discussed the research; they then paid home visits to assess the children, using the books used in that year's SATs and the running records used for assessment. The selected children were referred to as 'young early readers' (YERs). Following the assessment, the researchers contacted the primary schools that the selected children were to attend and with the help of teachers selected a control group, which they referred to as 'non young early readers' (NYERs). There were 15 children (10 girls and 5 boys in the YER group) and 14 children in the NYER group (as two of the former group were in the same school). Only two of 17 originally chosen left the area. The two groups were matched on a number of important variables; they were in the same class, of the same sex and of the same age; their scores on the vocabulary test were comparable and they were from the same socio-economic background. As far as possible they had similar preschool experiences. All the children were in two-parent families at the beginning of the research.

The progress of these 29 children was monitored from when they started school until the end of Key Stage 1. Reading, spelling and handwriting were assessed at yearly intervals; in reception class (or at home), in Year 1 and in Year 2; in Year 1 and Year 2 their compositional writing was assessed. Teachers and parents were interviewed each year, and at the end of the project each child was given a semi-structured interview. The results are presented in the book mainly in the form of case studies, with the children given pseudonyms.

The research confirmed the importance of the interrelatedness of alphabetic knowledge and phonological skills. There was evidence that the YERs had experienced many forms of print in their homes in addition to books, and had repeated interactions with adults. The teachers were, in the main, reasonably positive towards these children. However, it must be remembered that they knew throughout that the children's progress was being monitored, and knew just how advanced were the children's reading skills on entry. Some teachers managed to cater for the YERs' needs by lending books of their own and by engaging in dialogue with the individual children. However, as I had noted, teachers often found it a problem to provide appropriate reading materials. Also as I had found, the parents would have welcomed more school-initiated contact and reports on the children's progress; yet they were diffident about taking up the time of the teachers, or being seen as conceited because of their children's advanced reading skills.

> Because of the nature of these researches, in neither instance is it appropriate to deduce that there are more of either sex who begin school reading with fluency and understanding. It would be necessary to screen a large population for reading as they enter school, even including a sample in preschool units, to allow consideration of whether there are indeed sex differences.

Stainthorp and Hughes do not distinguish the reading materials that were of interest to the boys and girls in their research. I found a tendency for a number of the boys from an early age to be interested in non-fiction, information texts, which would be the most difficult for the children to access in the early stages at school.

RETROSPECTIVE AND CASE STUDIES

It is interesting to compare these two studies, undertaken 24 years apart, when in the intervening years there have been many changes in the teaching of reading and many researches of relevance to literacy. It is important to note that both studies, although they monitored the children's progress through the early stages in primary school, were retrospective, in the sense that the children were only identified after they could read with fluency. It seems appropriate to end this chapter with a further warning about deducing cause and effect from retrospective studies.

The young fluent readers in both researches were studied during their first few years in school; however, the information on the years before they entered school was 'retrospective' and depended on the parents' memory of events. All memory is selective, and what appears later to be of particular relevance may be influenced by subsequent events. For example, in a child who later develops a stutter, the child's hesitations in speech at an early age may acquire particular significance; while in a child who later becomes a fluent speaker these may not be remembered. Indeed in community studies of children's speech development it was found that such hesitations were a common feature in the early development of many normal children.

> A great deal of information in research, in case studies and in medical histories is collected retrospectively. While such information is important, it is crucial to appreciate its limitations; the likely biases that may be introduced. Check for information from large samples of children observed at an earlier stage.

It seems important to recognize the contribution of their home experiences to the success of the children discussed in this chapter, and to note that some of the schools might have accepted full credit and assumed that the success was directly attributable to the instruction they had provided had these children not been identified by these researches. Education neither begins at 5 years of age nor at 9.00 a.m. We are all too ready to attribute the failures to the homes but to claim the entire success for the school and formal education. At a time when there is so much stress on the value of preschool education and negative comparisons with children whose parents did not send them to a preschool, it is worth remembering that some parents make a conscious choice to educate their children at home. Two recent articles are relevant: the first compares children in the large EPPE study who did attend preschool with a home sample who did not (Sammons *et al.* 2004); the other article considers home-educated children, that is children who did not attend school during the reception stage (Rothermel 2004). Although the latter is an exploratory study it does remind us of the need to remember that there are parents who choose to educate their children 'otherwise' than by attending school, and to consider what we can learn from them.

Chapter 12

Better beginnings

In this book I have presented an analysis of some of the major researches evaluated in *Children Under Five; educational research and evidence* (Clark 1988). I have also included several of my researches from the previous edition of *Understanding Research in Early Education* (Clark 1989); this enables me to extend the discussion into the early years in the primary school. Recently completed and ongoing research is also considered. My aim is to encourage readers to see research as a continuous process.

It is worth identifying the extent to which the issues raised and warnings given over the years since 1988 are still of relevance for early education. In 1988 my evaluation of research relevant to the education of children under 5 years of age was published (Clark 1988). The following year there was a report from a House of Commons select committee, and a further select committee report in 2000 (House of Commons 1989 and in 2000). The report of the Rumbold Committee, *Starting with Quality*, was published in 1990 (DES 1990).

The following are among the issues that I identified in 1988.

- *In Britain, most children attend some form of educational provision before their fifth birthday.* Whether or not a particular child attends, what type of provision they attend, whether there is any choice and whether attendance is full time or part time will depend on the exact area in which the child lives, the child's precise date of birth and the parents' knowledge of available provision. Those children who attend day nurseries that provide all-day/ all-year care, many of whom have severe problems, may have frequent changes of carers and little access to a range of educational activities.
- *The staffing and other resources made available to those children admitted to primary school before the statutory age for entry differ widely.* It is dangerous to assume that early entry to primary school gives children a good start, unless the appropriate resources and skilled staff are available.
- *Access to education has already become unequal for young children by the time they reach the statutory age for starting school.* The effects could be further exacerbated unless the staffing in the early stages of the primary school is

sufficiently generous and well-qualified to make effective communication with young children possible. The staff must also be free from constraints that might prevent them from offering the young children sufficient breadth and depth of experiences.

- *It is possible from research evidence in homes and in preschool units to pinpoint contexts likely to stimulate learning in young children and to lay an effective foundation for literacy and numeracy.* Already by 5 years of age there are wide differences in the readiness of children for more-formal aspects of education and in their grasp of the underlying concepts on which to build numeracy and literacy.

- *Differences and changes in age of entry to primary school have important implications, both for the preschool services and for teachers of reception classes, some of whom may have children as young as 4 years of age, others over 5 years.* For some children entry to reception class in primary school is a transfer from one, or more than one, preschool setting in which a foundation has already been laid; for others it is their first experience away from home. Added to this, in some preschool units and in some reception classes, English may be an additional language for most of the children, not the language used in the home or one within which they are as yet competent. Furthermore, in some classes, there may be many different languages in use by the children, making dialogue between adults and children and between peers difficult to sustain.

- *The appropriate pace and range of experiences in both preschool education and reception class must vary to meet the children's stage of development and previous experiences.* A very different curriculum may be offered to children, even of the same age, depending on whether they happen to attend a preschool or reception class. Studies of transition also show that for some children the primary school may provide a less-stimulating and challenging experience than these same children had previously and to which they were responding; making meaningful choices, concentrating for long periods and engaging in dialogue with adults and sustained co-operation with peers.

- *Observational studies have shown that a free play setting has potential for stimulating learning in young children.* If it is to be an effective learning environment, particularly for the children in most need of support, it must be carefully structured, with the adults playing a crucial role in its organization and by selective intervention with children in their 'play'.

- *There is evidence of the language and cognitive tasks of which young children are capable, given appropriate contexts – and the need for greater challenge for some children.* Communication with adults that is meaningful, activities that make sense to the children and shared and challenging activities with peers are valuable in laying the foundation for children's educational development.

- *Some children come to school already well on the way to literacy and numeracy and able to communicate effectively with adults and peers.* The teachers who have such children in their class have a very different task from that of their colleagues.

- *Where the potential and present competence of young children is assessed by brief and formal contacts, for example in question and answer sessions, their present level of functioning and potential may be seriously underestimated and teacher expectations may colour their subsequent progress.* Furthermore, the less experience with adults the child has had, the greater the danger of underestimation. Even greater skill and sensitivity is required when assessing and helping children who have communication difficulties, either because of special educational needs or because they speak a language other than that of the staff.

- *Teachers of young children may find themselves under pressure to be 'seen' to be teaching to specific but limited targets.* To go 'back to the basics' would be disastrous if this ignores recent insights and results in children being deprived of a broad range of experiences in their early education. Some administrators, fellow teachers and, particularly, parents perceive 'good' early education in terms of 'work'(as opposed to 'play') and a narrowly interpreted programme of introduction to the basic skills at as early an age as possible. The ability to communicate effectively and creatively orally in meaningful contexts, to solve problems of increasing complexity, individually and collaboratively, are important foundations for young children's learning. It would be unfortunate if these are sacrificed in attempts to achieve short-term testable evidence of attainment.

Consider how many of these issues are still relevant and the extent to which research has provided evidence for policy-makers and practitioners.

The following three priorities, which I identified in 1988, still require further research:

- continuity of children's experiences between 3 and 7 or 8 years of age; with a focus on the curriculum and links between home and school
- expectations of parents from different cultural backgrounds; the extent to which they are similar to or different from those of the teachers and administrators
- needs of children in rural areas, which may have been neglected; the focus has been on deprivation in the inner cities and the effects of this on educational progress.

These are extracts from Chapter 18 of *Children Under Five: educational research and evidence* (Clark 1988).

Do you regard these as priorities for research? If so, what types of investigations do you think are needed?

The report of my investigation was consulted by the all-party Education, Science and the Arts Committee for its report *Educational Provision for the Under Fives* (House of Commons 1989). The Secretary of State's response to the publication of the report was to announce the establishment of a further committee, to be chaired by Angela Rumbold, to enquire into the quality of the educational experience offered to 3- and 4-year-olds. He commented that 'the national curriculum will introduce a new set of factors which those providing education for preschool children will need to take into account'. This was shortly after the passing of the Education Reform Act in 1988, and when controversy surrounded the curriculum recommendations of the various subject committees (Hansard 1989).

I expressed concern at the establishment of another committee, and the reasons given by the Secretary of State for taking that action. I argued that 'the quality, continuity and progression' sought by the Secretary of State should develop from the foundations of good early education, and not be dictated downwards by already prescribed guidelines within the National Curriculum; this view was also expressed by the select committee. It is interesting to observe how long it has taken for the term 'foundation' to be used in relation to early education!

In 1989 the all-party select committee stressed the importance of early education in its own right and as a foundation for the whole process of schooling (House of Commons 1989). There was no suggestion that preschool education should replace the central role of the parents, rather it should be complementary to and in keeping with the wishes of the parents. The importance of parents as educators and of building bridges between home and school was recognized.

A major section of the report was on quality provision, where it was emphasized that 'good quality provision for under fives should address both care and education' and that the aim should be 'to meet the child's intellectual, aesthetic, emotional physical and social development'.

- The importance of variety of provision was stressed, but also of ensuring that there was an educational input into all forms of preschool unit.
- It was felt that greater emphasis should be given to the status of nursery teachers. The committee showed its awareness of the importance of nursery nurses.
- Concern was expressed when early entry to reception class was used as a substitute for preschool education. Attention was drawn to the possible inappropriateness of the curriculum and the training of some of the teachers, and not least the inadequate adult : child ratio in many reception classes compared with preschool units.
- Finally concern was expressed at the proposed testing of children at 7 years of age.

During the intervening years some of the concerns expressed have proved to be justified. That not all its recommendations have borne fruit may be seen from the issues raised in the recent report by the Education and Employment Committee (House of Commons 2000). Its remit was to consider the appropriate content of early years education: the way it should be taught, the kinds of staff who should teach it, the way quality of teaching and learning in the early years should be assessed and the age at which formal schooling should start. The age range with which it was concerned was broad: 3 years old up to Year 1 of primary school. The following are its main recommendations.

- The role of the parents as vital educators of their children should be given prominence. They should also be encouraged to help practitioners to draw up individual profiles for their children.
- Birth to 5 years should be regarded as the first phase of education, and since education and care are inseparable there should be a universal service under the leadership of a single government department. There should be increased funding for Sure Start and Early Excellence Centres. Children below compulsory school age should be taught informally in ways that are appropriate to their developmental age and interests.
- Structured learning should be introduced very gradually, so that even by the end of the reception year children are learning through more-formal, whole-class activities for a small proportion of the day. Thus support was given to the report on the Foundation Stage (QCA/DfEE 2000), which should be regarded as providing illustrations, rather than stepping stones, for a child from age 3 years to the end of the Foundation Stage.
- The importance of children's personal, social and emotional development is stressed.
- Every setting outside a home that offers early education should have a trained teacher on the staff; their training should emphasize not only the skills of working with children, but also those of working with adults. There should be expanded training opportunities in the voluntary and private sectors, and trained teachers involved in the networks supporting childminders.
- In reception classes and in Year 1 the adult : child ratio should be no more than 15 : 1.
- Recommendations are made concerning the qualifications in care and education of young children which should be required of the OfSTED Director of Early Years and the staff.

Concerns expressed by early educators are addressed, and the recommendations appear to endorse many of the Government's recent initiatives.

Since 1989 numerous reports with implications for early years have been published; in England these have had changing, even conflicting, recommendations. *Starting with Quality* (DES 1990), the report of the Rumbold

Committee, was strongly influenced by the views of early educators, some of whom were members of the committee. However, over the intervening years some of the concerns expressed have been justified, with a backwash effect on early education from the National Curriculum in England; in particular the assessment of children's progress by SATs at the end of Key Stage 1, when some of the children were barely 7 years of age and with wide differences in the lengths of time they had been at school. The introduction of compulsory Baseline Assessment in England concerned early educators, particularly as one purpose for its introduction seemed to be as a basis for measurement of the 'value-added' by schools during each Key Stage.

Although 'education and care' are among the powers devolved to the Scottish Parliament and Welsh Assembly, and terminology may vary, many of the current trends in preschool education and care are similar. Integration of services, combined services with a focus on the needs of families, provision of out-of-hours, wrap-around care, based in schools, and training of professionals, particularly for leadership; all are important political topics. It appears that the Government is now committed to the massive additional expenditure needed for their recommendations to be implemented.

During recent years there have been no serious proposals to make preschool education compulsory or to lower (or raise) the age for starting statutory education; the latest age in England currently being the term after the child's fifth birthday, and in Scotland the beginning of the school year if the child will be 5 years of age by the end of February. There has, however, been a massive increase in the availability of preschool education and care for children aged 3 and 4 years of age, with provision for all children whose parents wish it for them. More attention is now directed to issues of quality within different types of preschool provision. In Scotland there is an emphasis in recent publications on self-evaluation, with associated materials including videos to facilitate discussion. *The Child at the Centre: self-evaluation in the early years* is one example of such publications (Scottish Executive 2000). A recent publication by the National Audit Office, *Early Years: progress in developing high quality childcare and early education accessible to all* (NAO 2004), addresses this issue. The report states that although there are many more childcare places available for preschool children, there are gaps in provision for some groups and in some geographical areas; there is less early-years provision in the most deprived areas. It is also noted that further improvements to accessibility and quality will depend on a faster expansion of the workforce involved in early education and childcare.

There are a number of initiatives planned to assist practitioners assess and improve the quality of learning in their centres; one example is the Effective Early Learning (EEL) projects developed by CREC (which has added a BabyEEL). Evaluations of Early Excellence Centres (EECs) have also been conducted by CREC (Bertram *et al.* 2002 and 2004). The second report of the National Evaluation of Sure Start (NESS) team, *Fathers in Sure Start*

(Lloyd et al. 2003), has focused on a neglected area within early education research; often when the term 'parent' is used it actually refers to the mother. This study revealed a strong maternal focus in many services and a need to involve fathers and to make the environments 'male friendly'. Good leadership is essential if quality is to be improved. In an article based on a literature review it is claimed that so far there is little high-quality research on leadership in early childhood (Muijs *et al.* 2004). One initiative, developed by Margy Whalley and her team at Pen Green Centre, has recently been launched; this will provide nationally recognized leadership qualifications for those working in multi-disciplinary environments across education, health and social services. EPPE, a major longitudinal research funded by DfES (referred to extensively earlier), and its related studies consider the long-term effects of preschool education and aim to identify the features within centres that facilitate learning (see pages 78–80).

Attention is now turning to the education and care of children under 3 years old. In England there has been the publication of *Birth to Three Matters: a framework to support children in their earliest years* (DfES/Sure Start 2002). In Scotland, after extensive consultation by the Scottish Executive Education Department (SEED) the report *Birth to Three: supporting our youngest children* has been published, together with a supporting booklet for parents (LTS 2005).

The National Curriculum in England and Wales and SATs have probably adversely affected the curriculum offered to children in the early years in primary school, and probably had a backwash effect on the curriculum offered to children under 5 years of age. In Wales SATs have been abolished from the end of Key Stage 1, and in 2004 the format has been changed in England following pilot studies, with greater flexibility and more emphasis on teacher assessment; thus league tables are less likely to hang over the heads of early educators. In Scotland, the *Curriculum Framework for Children 3–5* (SCCC 1999) links with the National Guidelines 5–14; a review of the curriculum 3–18 is currently underway. In England the Curricular Guidelines for the Foundation Stage apply only until children reach statutory age for starting school (until the end of reception class), although this may be extended. In Wales the Foundation Phase lasts until the end of Year 1, that is a further year. Baseline Assessment in England, which was of concern to early educators as it took place very early in a child's attendance in school, has now been replaced by the Foundation Stage Profile, based on observation of the child and over a longer period (QCA/DfES 2003). Baseline Assessment has never been compulsory in Scotland; however, a number of local authorities have chosen to introduce some form of baseline assessment.

If, as seems likely, preschool education remains voluntary, there will be children whose first experience of 'formal' education is when they reach statutory age for starting school. Insufficient attention has been paid to such children in official reports, and the danger that making assessments too early may underestimate their potential because of their limited interactions by that stage with 'strange' adults.

Too little attention has been paid to how to relate to parents, who may have very different views on appropriate educational experiences for their young children from those informing the practices in schools, preschool and primary. This is particularly a matter of concern in multicultural Britain, where English is an additional language for many children, indeed for most children in some inner-city schools.

The Government is now committed to providing preschool education for all 3- and 4-year-olds whose parents wish it, to ensuring quality in the curriculum offered, and to considering the needs of children from birth to 3 years. Only lip service has so far been paid to continuity of children's learning experiences; 'transition' would still be a more appropriate term for what has been studied, with only the point of transition varying. We must now give priority to ensuring continuity within early educational experiences of all children, with co-operation between the professionals and partnership with the parents.

References

Note: It seemed important to provide an extended reference list, although I appreciate that many of the earlier publications are now out of print. Many are still cited, and from time to time new editions of some of the research reports and texts appear.

> Research and teaching were linked throughout my career and I encouraged students, many of whom were practitioners in early years settings, to link their dissertations to ongoing funded research and to write articles for publication. I thought those of you who are studying might find it encouraging to see the references to students' dissertations and related articles to which I referred in the text; these I have marked with an asterisk.

Ahmad, K. (1986) 'The language of young Punjabi speaking children on starting school', unpublished dissertation, Faculty of Education, University of Birmingham.★

Ashton, C. (2004) 'Our children deserve better', *Education Review: educating the whole child*, 17(2): 24–8.

Aubrey, C. (2004) 'Implementing the foundation stage in reception classes', *British Educational Research Journal*, 30(5): 633–56.

Aubrey, C., David, T., Godfrey, R. *et al.* (2000) *Early Childhood Educational Research: issues in methodology and ethics*, London: RoutledgeFalmer.

Aubrey, C., Godfrey, R. and Godfrey, J. (2000) 'Children's early numeracy experiences at home', *Primary Practice*, 26(Sept.): 36–42.

Barrett, G. (1986) *Starting School: an evaluation of the experience*, AMMA, Norwich: University of East Anglia.

Bennett, N. and Kell, J. (1989) *A Good Start? Four year olds in infant schools*, Oxford: Blackwell.

BERA (British Education Research Association: Early Years Special Interest Group) (2003) *Early Years Research: pedagogy, curriculum and adult roles, training and professionalism*, Southwell: BERA.

Bernstein, B. (1970) 'A sociological approach to socialization with some reference to educability', in F. Williams (ed.) *Language and Poverty: perspectives on a theme*, Chicago: Markham Publ. Co.

— (2003) *Basil Bernstein: Class, codes and control*, 4 vols. Reprint of works published between 1971–1990, London: RoutledgeFalmer.

Bertram, T., Pascal, C., Bokhari, S., Gasper, M. and Holtermann, S. (2002) *Early Excellence Centre Pilot Programme: second evaluation report 2000–2001* (DfES Research Report 361), London: DfES.

Bertram, T., Pascal, C., Bokhari, S., Gasper, M., Holtermann, S. and Nelson, C. (2004) *Early Excellence Centres Pilot Programme: third annual evaluation report, 2001–2002*, London: DfES.

Bissex, G.L. (1980) *GNYS AT WRK: a child learns to write and read*, Cambridge, MA: Harvard University Press.

Blank, M. (1985) 'Classroom discourse: the neglected topic of the topic', in M.M. Clark (ed.) *Helping Communication in Early Education*, Educational Review Occasional Publications 11, Birmingham: University of Birmingham.

Blank, M., Rose, S.A. and Berlin, L. (1978a) *Preschool Language Assessment Instrument*, New York: Grune and Stratton.

— (1978b) *The Language of Learning: the preschool years*, New York: Grune and Stratton.

Blatchford, P., Battle, S. and Mays. M. (1982) *The First Transition: home to preschool*, Windsor: NFER-Nelson.

Bogle, M. (1985) 'The meaning component in language learning in early education', in M.M. Clark (ed.) *Helping Communication in Early Education*, Educational Review Occasional Pubications 11, Birmingham: University of Birmingham.

Broadhead, P. (ed.) (1996) *Researching the Early Years Continuum*, Clevedon: Multilingual Matters.

Bruner, J. (1980) *Under Five in Britain*, London: Grant McIntyre.

Bryce, T.G.K. and Humes, W.M. (eds) (2003) *Scottish Education: second edition post-devolution*, Edinburgh: Edinburgh University Press (first edition 1999).

Butler, D. (1975) *Cushla and her Books*, Auckland: Hodder and Stoughton.

Cazden, C.B. (1970) 'The neglected situation in child language research and education', in F. Williams (ed.) *Language and Poverty: perspectives on a theme*, Chicago: Markham Publ. Co.

— (1977) 'Concentrated versus contrived encounters: suggestions for language assessment in early childhood', in A. Davies (ed.) *Language and Learning in Early Childhood*, London: Heinemann.

Clark, M.M. (1970) *Reading Difficulties in Schools*, Harmondsworth: Penguin (new edition 1979, Heinemann).

— (1976) *Young Fluent Readers: what can they teach us?*, London: Heinemann.

— (1984) 'Literacy at home and at school: insights from a study of young fluent readers', in H. Goelman, A. Oberg and F. Smith (eds) *Awakening to Literacy*, Exeter, NH: Heinemann.

— (ed.) (1985a) *Helping Communication in Early Education*, Educational Review, Occasional Publications 11, Birmingham: University of Birmingham.

— (ed.) (1985b) *New Directions in the Study of Reading*, Lewes: Falmer Press.

— (1988) *Children Under Five: educational research and evidence*, London: Gordon and Breach.

— (1989) *Understanding Research in Early Education*, London: Gordon and Breach.

— (1994) *Young Literacy Learners: how we can help them*, Leamington Spa: Scholastic.

— (2002) 'Teaching assistants: their role in the primary schools of the future', *Primary Practice*, 31, Summer: 18–20.

— (2003) 'Education in Scotland: what can we learn from the census?' *Primary Practice*, 35, Autumn: 31–3.

— (2004) 'Education in England and Wales: what can we learn from the census?' *Primary Practice*, 36, Spring: 35–8.

Clark, M.M., Barr, J.E. and Dewhirst, W. (1984) *Education of Children with Communication Problems: particularly those from ethnic minorities*, Report of DES research, Offset Publication 3, Birmingham: University of Birmingham.

Clark, M.M. and Cheyne, W.M. (eds) (1979) *Studies in Preschool Education*, London: Hodder and Stoughton.

Clark, M.M. and Munn, P. (eds) (1997) *Education in Scotland: policy and practice from pre-school to secondary*, London: Routledge.

Clay, M.M. (1972) *Reading: the patterning of complex behaviour*, Auckland: Heinemann.

— (1991) *Becoming Literate: the construction of inner control*, Auckland: Heinemann.

Cleave, S., Jowett, S. and Bate, M. (1982) *And So To School: a study of continuity from preschool to infant school*, Windsor: NFER.

Close, R. (2004) 'Television and early language', *Education Journal*, Issue 77: 29 (the full research review can be downloaded from www.literacytrust.org).

Coates, E.A. (1985) 'An examination of the nature of young children's discussions, both in peer groups and with an adult', in M.M. Clark (ed.) *Helping Communication in Early Education*, Educational Review Occasional Publication 11, Birmingham: University of Birmingham.★

Davenport, E. (1983) 'The play of Sikh children in a nursery school and at home', *Educational Review*, 35(2): 127–140.★

Davidson, J. (2004) 'Wales: the learning country', *Education Review: educating the whole child*, 17(2): 3–8.

Davie, C.E., Hutt, S.J., Vincent, E. *et al.* (1984) *The Young Child at Home*, Windsor: NFER/Nelson.

Davies, A. (ed.) (1977) *Language and Learning in Early Childhood*, London: Heinemann.

Davies, B., Muller, J. and Morais, A. (eds) (2004) *Reading Bernstein, Researching Bernstein*, London: RoutledgeFalmer.

DES (Department of Education and Science) (1967) *Children and their Primary Schools*, vols 1 and 2, The Plowden Report, London: HMSO.

— (1975a) *A Language for Life*, The Bullock Report, London: HMSO.

— (1975b) *Preschool Education and Care: some topics requiring research or development projects*, London: DES.

— (1990) *Starting with Quality: Report of the Rumbold Committee*, London: HMSO.

DfES (Department for Education and Skills)/Sure Start Unit (2002) *Birth to Three Matters: a framework to support children in their earliest years*, London: DfES.

Dewhirst, W. (1985) 'Settings as contexts for dialogue: guidelines for practice in the management and organisation of communication between children', in M.M. Clark (ed.) *Helping Communication in Early Education*, Educational Review Occasional Publications 11, Birmingham: University of Birmingham.

Donachy, W. (1976) 'Parental participation in preschool education', *British Journal of Educational Psychology*, 46: 31–9.★

— (1979) 'Parental participation in preschool education', in M.M. Clark and W.M. Cheyne (eds) *Studies in Preschool Education*, London: Hodder and Stoughton.★

Donaldson, M. (1978) *Children's Minds*, Glasgow: Fontana/Collins.

— (1984) 'Speech and writing and modes of learning', in H. Goelman, A. Oberg. and F. Smith (eds) *Awakening to Literacy*, Exeter, NH: Heinemann.

Dunlop, A-W. and Fabian, H. (eds) (2003) *Transitions*, Themed Monographs Series 1, European Childhood Research Journal, Worcester: EECERA.

Ferreiro, E. (1984) 'The underlying logic of literacy development', in H. Goelman, A. Oberg and F. Smith (eds) *Awakening to Literacy*, Exeter, NH: Heinemann.

Goelman, H., Oberg, A. and Smith, F. (eds) (1984) *Awakening to Literacy*, Exeter, NH: Heinemann.

Gregory, E., Williams, A., Baker, D. *et al.* (2004) 'Introducing literacy to four year olds: creating classroom cultures in three schools', *Journal of Early Childhood Literacy*, vol. 4(1): 85–107.

Greig, A. and Taylor, J. (1999) *Doing Research with Children*, London: Sage.

Hall, N., Jarson, J. and Marsh, J. (eds) (2003) *Handbook of Early Childhood Literacy*, London: Sage.

Hansard (1989) 'Debate on preschool education and care', 18 January: 401.

Hart, B. and Risley, T.R. (1995) *Meaningful Differences in the Everyday Experience of Young American Children*, Baltimore: Paul Brookes. (Third printing, 2002, has new preface.)

House of Commons (1989) *Educational Provision for the Under Fives*, vols I and II, Report of the Education, Science and Arts Committee, London: HMSO.

— (2000) *Early Years*, vols I and II, Report of the Education and Employment Committee, London: HMSO.

— (2004/5) 'The Teaching of Reading', an enquiry by the Education and Skills Committee, uncorrected oral evidence from 8 December 2004 and 7 February 2005, unpublished.

Hunt, J.McV. (1961) *Intelligence and Experience*, New York: Ronald Press.

— (1969) *The Challenge of Incompetence and Poverty: papers on the role of early education*, Urbana: University of Illinois Press.

Hutt, S.J., Tyler, S., Hutt, C. and Foy, H. (1984) 'A natural history of the preschool, Final Report to DES', unpublished.

Hutt, S.J., Tyler, S., Hutt, C. and Christopherson, H. (1989) *Play, Exploration and Learning: a natural history of the preschool*, London: Routledge.

Katz, L.C. (1985) 'Fostering communicative competence in young children', in M.M. Clark (ed.) *Helping Communication in Early Education*, Educational Review Occasional Publications 11, Birmingham: University of Birmingham.

Labov, W. (1970) 'The Logic of Nonstandard English', in F. Williams (ed.) *Language and Poverty: perspectives on a theme*, Chicago: Markham Publ. Co.

Lindsay, G. and Lewis, A. (2003) 'An evaluation of the use of accredited baseline assessment schemes in England', *British Educational Research Journal*, 29(2): 149–67.

Lindsay, G., Martineau, E. and Lewis, A. (2004) 'The consistency of baseline assessment schemes as measures of early literacy', *Journal of Research in Reading*, 27(2): 118–31.

Lloyd, N., O'Brien, M. and Lewis, C. (2003) *Fathers in Sure Start*. National Evaluation of Sure Start Implementation Report No. 2, London: DfES.

Lomax, C.M. (1977) 'Interest in books and stories at nursery school', *Educational Research*, 19: 100–12.

— (1979) 'Studies in Dunbartonshire nurseries', in M.M. Clark and W.M. Cheyne (eds) *Studies in Preschool Education*, London: Hodder and Stoughton.

LTS (Learning and Teaching Scotland) (2005) *Birth to Three: supporting our youngest children*, Dundee: Learning and Teaching Scotland.

Marsh, J. (ed.) (2005) *Popular Culture, New Media and Digital Literacy in Early Childhood*, London: RoutledgeFalmer.

Melhuish, E., Sylva, K., Sammons, P., Siraj-Blatchford, I., Taggart, B., Dobson, A., Jeavons, M., Lewis, K., Morahan, M. and Sadler, S. (1999) *Parent, Family and Child Characteristics in Relation to Type of Pre-school and Socio-economic Differences*, Technical Paper 4, EPPE Project, London: Institute of Education.

Muijs, D., Aubrey, C., Harris, A. and Briggs, M. (2004) 'How do they manage? A review of the research on leadership in early childhood', *Journal of Early Childhood*, 2(2): 157–69.

NAO (National Audit Office) (2004) *Early Years: progress in developing high quality childcare and early education accessible to all*, London: HMSO.

Nisbet, J. and Watt, J. (1984) *Educational Disadvantage: ten years on*, Edinburgh: HMSO.

— (1994) *Educational Disadvantage in Scotland: a 1990s perspective*, Edinburgh: Scottish Community Education Council.

Payne, G. (1985) 'Planning activities that will provide appropriate contexts to promote adult–child and child–child communication in the nursery unit', in M.M. Clark (ed.) *Helping Communication in Early Education*, Educational Review Occasional Publications 11, Birmingham: University of Birmingham.★

Payton, S. (1984) *Developing Awareness of Print*, Educational Review, Offset Publications 2, Birmingham: University of Birmingham.★

Pearson, S.A. (1987) 'Language Interaction Between Child–Child and Adult–Child among Moslem Children who are about to Transfer from Nursery School to Infant School', unpublished dissertation, Faculty of Education, University of Birmingham.★

Pugh, G. (ed.) (2001) *Contemporary Issues in the Early Years: working collaboratively for children*, London: Paul Chapman.

QCA (Qualifications and Curriculum Authority)/DfEE (2000) *Curriculum Guidance for the Foundation Stage*, London: QCA.

QCA/DfES (2003) *The Foundation Stage Profile*, London: QCA.

Robinson, W.P. (1980) 'Language management, socio-economic status and educational progress', in L.A. Hersov and M. Berger (eds) *Language and Language Disorders in Early Childhood*, New York: Pergamon Press.

Robson, B. (1983a) 'Encouraging dialogue in preschool units: the role of the pink pamfer', *Educational Review*, 35(2): 141–8.★

— (1983b) 'Encouraging interaction between staff and children with communication problems in preschool units', in M.M. Clark (ed.) *Special Educational Needs and Children Under Five*, Educational Review Occasional Publication 9, Birmingham: University of Birmingham.★

— (1989) *Special Needs in Ordinary Schools: pre-school provision for children with special needs*, London: Cassell.★

Rothermel, P. (2004) 'Home-education comparison of home- and school-educated children on PIPs baseline assessments', *Journal of Early Childhood Research*, 2(3): 273–99.

Sammons, P., Elliot, K., Sylva, K., Melhuish, E., Siraj-Blatchford, I. and Taggart, B. (2004) The impact of pre-school on young children's cognitive attainments at entry to reception, *British Journal of Educational Research*, 30(5): 691–707.

Sammons, P., Sylva, K., Melhuish, E., Siraj-Blatchford, I., Taggart, B. and Elliot, K. (2002) *Measuring the Impact of Pre-school on Children's Cognitive Progress over the Pre-school Period*, Technical Paper 8a, EPPE Project, London: Institute of Education.

Sanders, D., White, G., Burge, B., Sharp, C., Eames, A., McEune, R. and Grayson, H. (2005) *A Study of Transition from the Foundation Stage to Key Stage 1*, DfES Research Report, London: DfES.

Schaffer, H.R. (1990) *Making Decisions about Children: psychological questions and answers*, Oxford: Basil Blackwell.

SCCC (Scottish Consultative Council on the Curriculum) (1999) *Curriculum Framework for Children 3 to 5*, Dundee: SCCC (now available from Learning and Teaching Scotland, which has replaced SCCC, see www.LTScotland.org.uk).

Scottish Executive (2000) *The Child at the Centre: self-evaluation in the early years*, Edinburgh: Scottish Executive.

Shinman, S.M. (1981) *A Chance for Every Child: access and response to preschool provision*, London: Tavistock.

Shorrocks, D. (1995) 'Evaluating National Curriculum Assessment at Key Stage 1: retrospect and prospect', in P. Broadhead (ed.) *Researching the Early Years Continuum*, Clevedon: Multilingual Matters.

Siraj-Blatchford, I. and Sylva, K. (2004) 'Researching pedagogy in English pre-schools', *British Educational Research Journal*, 30(5): 713–30.

Siraj-Blatchford, I., Taggart, B., Sylva, K., Melhuish, E. and Sammons, P. (2004) 'Effective Pre-school and Primary Education (EPPE 3-11), *Primary Practice*, 37, Summer: 28–30.

Smith, F. (1971) *Understanding Reading*, New York: Hart, Rinehart and Winston.

Southgate, V. and Roberts, G.R (1970) *Reading – Which Approach?*, London: University of London Press.

Stainthorp, R. and Hughes, D. (1999) *Learning from Children who Read at an Early Age*, London: Routledge.

— (2004) 'What happens to precocious readers' performance by the age of eleven?' *Journal of Research in Reading*, 27(4): 357–72.

Sutton, W. (1985) 'Some factors in pre-school children of relevance to learning to read', in M.M. Clark (ed.) *New Directions in the Study of Reading*, Lewes: Falmer Press.★

Sylva, K., Melhuish, E.C., Sammons, P., Siraj-Blatchford, I. and Taggart, B. (2004a) *The Effective Provision of Pre-school Education (EPPE) Project. Technical Paper 12 – The Final Report: Effective Pre-school Education*, London: DfES/Institute of Education, University of London.

— (2004b) *The Effective Provision of Pre-School (EPPE) Project: findings from pre-school to end of Key Stage 1*, London. DfES/Sure Start.

Sylva, K., Roy, C. and Painter, M. (1980) *Childwatching at Playgroup and Nursery School*, London: Grant McIntyre.

Tizard, B., Blatchford, P., Burke, F., Farquhar, C. and Plewis, I. (1988) *Young Children at School in the Inner City*, Hove: Lawrence Erlbaum.

Tizard, B., Carmichael, H., Hughes, M. and Pinkerton, G. (1980) 'Four year olds talking to mothers and teachers', in L.A. Hersov and M. Berger (eds) *Language and Language Disorders in Childhood*, Oxford: Pergamon Press.

Tizard, B. and Hughes, M. (1984) *Young Children Learning: talking and thinking at home and at school*, London: Fontana (second edition with foreword by Judy Dunn was published in 2002, Oxford: Blackwell).

Tizard, B., Hughes, M., Carmichael, H. and Pinkerton, G. (1983a) 'Children's questions and adults' answers', *Journal of Child Psychology and Psychiatry*, 24(2): 269–81.

— (1983b) 'Language and social class: is verbal deprivation a myth?', *Journal of Child Psychology and Psychiatry*, 24(4): 533–42.

Tizard, H., Hughes, M., Pinkerton, G. and Carmichael, H. (1982) 'Adults' cognitive demands at home and at nursery school', *Journal of Child Psychology and Psychiatry*, 23(2): 105–16.

Tobin, J.J., Wu, D.Y.H. and Davidson, D.H. (1989) *Preschool in Three Cultures: Japan, China and the United States*, New Haven: Yale University Press.

Tough, J. (1977) *The Development of Meaning: a study of children's use of language*, London: Allen Unwin.

Toynbee, P. (2004) 'We can break the vice of the great unmentionable', *The Guardian*, 2 January: 8.

Van Lierop, M. (1985) 'Predisposing factors in early literacy: a case study', in M.M. Clark (ed.) *New Directions in the Study of Reading*, Lewes: Falmer Press.★

Wallace, F. (1985) 'The Aims of Nursery Education as Perceived by Headteachers of Nursery Schools and Teachers with Posts of Responsibility for Reception Children in Large Primary Schools', unpublished dissertation, Faculty of Education, University of Birmingham.★

Watt, J. (1987 'Continuity in early education', in M.M. Clark (ed.) *Roles, Responsibilities and Relationships in the Education of the Young Child*, Educational Review Occasional Publications 13, Birmingham: University of Birmingham.

Watt, J. and Flett, M. (1985), *Continuity in Early Education: the role of the parents*, Aberdeen: University of Aberdeen.

Wells, G. (1977) 'Language use and educational success: a response to Joan Tough's The Development of Meaning 1977', unpublished paper presented at the Child Language Saminar, Nottingham.

— (1985) *Language Development in the Preschool Years*, Cambridge: Cambridge University Press.

— (1986) *The Meaning Makers: children learning through language and using language to learn*, New Hampshire: Heinemann.

Whitehead, M.R. (1990; 3rd edn 2004) *Language and Literacy in the Early Years*, London: Sage.

Whittaker, H.M. (1985) 'The Assessment of Language Competence in Young Punjabi-English Speaking Children', unpublished dissertation, Faculty of Education, University of Birmingham.★

Williams, F. (ed.) (1970) *Language and Poverty: perspectives on a theme*, Chicago: Markham Pub. Co.

Wood, D., McMahon, L. and Cranstoun, Y. (1980) *Working with Under Fives*, London: Grant McIntyre.

Wood, D., Wood, H., Griffith, A. and Howarth, I. (1986) *Teaching and Talking with Deaf Children*, Chichester: Wiley.

Appendix I: Interview schedule for teachers of reception classes

From Research on Early Education and Children from Ethnic Minorities (discussed in Chapter 9)

This schedule formed the basis for the interviews of the reception class teachers who had been responsible for the children in the research discussed in chapters 8 and 9. Similar interviews were conducted with the teachers in charge of the infant departments and the teachers in the Ethnic Minority Support Service (EMSS).

> You should note that we were working with a small number of schools, five only, and nine reception class teachers. Thus the interview did not require to be so tightly structured as in some of my other researches where the responses of a large sample had to be analysed. Furthermore, by the time we interviewed the teachers we knew them well, and also knew a great deal about their classroom practices and their children's ability. Finally, all interviews were conducted by the same researcher, who was known to the teachers and was an expert in early education.

The interview began with rather general open-ended questions to get the teachers' spontaneous responses. At a later stage more specific questions were asked to ensure that the main topics were covered and that specific children were named where appropriate.

Introduction of the interview to the teachers:

We are interested in the perceptions you had of your reception children last year: how you saw them entering and then leaving your class; what you felt were the key areas in your curriculum aims; and if this class was any different or similar to classes you had taught before; if so, how?

AIMS

- What do you see as the *priorities* in being a reception teacher?
- What features helped you achieve your aims? (physical, human, curriculum)

- What other features constrained your practice?
- What range of entry skills did the reception children bring with them on entry?
- How did you go about building on them?
- What were your greatest successes? In which ways were you unsuccessful?
- If you were starting now, in what ways would you have done things differently? (materials, organization, approaches)
- What were the constraints preventing you from succeeding?
- Were there any particular features peculiar to last year affecting your teaching/learning context?
- Was there any child/children who had highly specific individual learning needs/problems?
- In relation to your aims as a reception teacher:
  a What do you see as the strengths/weaknesses of family grouping? (asked only in school which was family grouped)
  b If you had had a class of all reception children would it have altered the overall aims in the classroom?
- In relation to your aims as a reception teacher, what do you see as the strengths of:
  a three intakes a year?
  b one intake a year?
- In relation to your aims as a reception teacher:
  a What do you see as the strengths and weaknesses of a class of all reception children?
  b What about alternatives?
- What had you hoped to achieve with most of the children in the curriculum at the end of their reception year?
- In what ways do you see a difference between the reception class and a pre-reception class? Are there any similarities?
- Some children enter reception class having had a nursery class or school experience, some have not. Do you see them as having different needs? In what ways?

It has been suggested in recent research that children in nursery schools and classes have free choice of activities for most of the day.

- For what proportion of the day in the reception class do you consider children should have choice of activities? What sorts of activities?

The same study has suggested children in the nursery setting are free to move around at choice.

- What is your view about this for the *reception child*?
- To what extent did this happen in your reception class? For what purposes?

Research has also shown that nursery children are allowed to develop and sustain areas of interest/activity.

- To what extent is this appropriate in a reception class?
- What sorts of activities/areas/interest do children initiate as areas of interest?

TEACHER MOBILITY

In preschool, staff tend to move around and make contact and work with individual children for most of the day.

- How far do you think this is appropriate in the reception class?

PLAY/WORK

It has been observed through research that *play* was used as a label more often than *work* in the nursery setting, whereas *work* was used more in reception classes and *play* as something to do when work has been finished.

- How do you feel about this?

BASIC SKILLS

I expect that, like most teachers, you see helping children to read as part of the job of the reception class teacher.

- What kind of resources do you feel are important in helping you achieve this?
- Are there resources that you feel are important which you feel are in short supply?
- How do you decide when to start the teaching of reading with individual children?
- How do you go about it? (groups, individuals)
- What do you see as the early stages of *reading*?
- What do you see as the early stages of *writing*?
- What do you see as the early stages of *number*?

- Do you see a role for writing production as distinct from copy writing? If so, what?
- What is the role of story telling?

Have you read the research report *And so to School* [this was asked here as the earlier references to 'a research' were from its findings]?

- If you had been the teacher receiving the children into the next class, what skills would you have expected them to have in reading? ... in writing? ... in numeracy?
- Would you have expected this of all children?

ORAL LANGUAGE

We have talked about children, the curriculum and skills.

- What do you see as the importance of oral language?
- I expect some of the children have limitations in oral language on entry to reception class – which features are particularly striking?
- How much is it your responsibility to overcome these?
- Were there children whose language was so limited that it made it difficult for them to function in school? Who were they?
- In what ways were they experiencing difficulties?
- Were there any children you regarded as language-advanced and you had difficulties in catering for their needs within the constraints of the classroom?
- Do you feel that any of the children had particular difficulties because of their ethnic background?
- Language difficulties or problems in other areas – e.g. playground? What kinds of problems?

I know we have asked a lot of questions – perhaps we have asked the wrong ones. Are there any other points you want to raise that you think are relevant or important?

Appendix 2: Parental interview on early education

From Research on Early Education and Children from Ethnic Minorities (Clark, Barr and Dewhirst 1984) (discussed in Chapter 9)

The parents of some of the children who had been studied during their first year in school were interviewed. Most parents interviewed were either of Asian or Afro-Caribbean ethnic origin. Parents whose mother tongue was Punjabi were interviewed in that language by one of my students whose mother tongue was also Punjabi (see also Whittaker 1985). Similar topics were covered in interviews conducted subsequently by another student, also in Punjabi. These were of parents whose children were in nursery school and about to enter reception class (Ahmad 1986).

The topics listed below were covered at some point during the interview where possible, or adapted as appropriate. Some of the items were included only where the child's mother tongue was Punjabi and/or replaced by alternative items on background. The interviews were recorded for later transcription, and if necessary translation.

Although 'he' is used here, the same questions were asked concerning boys and girls; in each case, the child's name was used.

Name of child .... Person(s) interviewed ....

HOME BACKGROUND

- Children: position in family; age and sex of siblings; schools attended by siblings and whether nursery school attended.
- Number of adults in home.
- Mother and father: place of birth/date of arrival in UK/education, place and medium of instruction/age on leaving school/present work.
- Any holidays on subcontinent?
- Why was this area chosen to live? How long have you been living here?
- Do any relatives live nearby, if so do you visit each other frequently?

- Does anyone visit frequently who only speaks a language other than English?
- How often are you able to visit relatives?

LANGUAGE

(Where language of home is not English)

- Which language do you tend to use at home?
  a   adults
  b   adults and children
  c   children
  d   children with adults
- Any circumstances when other languages are used?
- Are you literate in first language (e.g. newspaper)?
- If yes, is that due to subcontinent schooling or something else, e.g. supplementary classes/home tuition in UK?
- Are any of the children learning to read/write first language? If so, at home or at classes? If not yet, will you encourage this when the children are older?
- Do your children have access to books, newspapers in first language, either adult or children's material?
- Does anyone read/tell stories to children in first language?
- If yes, how often? How is it done: with/without books or pictures?
- Do you feel the children benefit from the above?
- Do the children watch a lot of television? (special programmes)
- What sort of things has he learnt from television?
- What about films or videos? Have you got or do you hire a video recorder to watch Asian films? If yes, how often? If yes, do children watch as a family?
- Perhaps this has not been possible yet, but do you think children visiting the subcontinent is important?

LANGUAGE IN CONTEXT

- How do you think X's [name used] education is developing?
- How is he finding English and Punjabi?
- How do you feel about first language in school? Would you like to see it introduced? How? Why do you think it has not been introduced?

To Afro-Caribbean ethnic origin parents, questions were asked on the use of Creole/patois by themselves and the children.

PARENTAL PERCEPTIONS OF SCHOOLING

- How do you feel X [name used] is getting on at school?
- What kinds of things do you think he is learning? Are there other things you would have liked him to learn?
- Did he settle in school straight away?
- Does he talk to you about school? What kinds of things does he talk about?
- Does he have special friends at school? Have you met any of them?
- Who does he play with when not at school?
- What does he play at? Also when he is alone?
- Did you enjoy being at school? Age on leaving? Did you study afterwards?
- How important do you think education is for your child?

HOME–SCHOOL LINKS

- How often do you go to school? Welcome?
- Do you ever get a chance to talk to the teacher?
- Have you ever had a chance to be in the classroom?
- Would you like to have had the chance?
- Did you find it interesting?
- What are the ways you feel you can best help your child to get on in school?

CHILD AT HOME

- Do you think it is important for your child to read?
- Do you have time to read yourself? If so, what?
- Do you take a newspaper regularly?
- Does he like to play with other children? If there are no other children what does he do?
- Is he like his brothers and sisters?
- Does he get upset easily?
- Do you have to check his behaviour often/not often/hardly ever?
- What kinds of things does he talk about?
- What does he particularly enjoy doing?
- Does he watch television? Special programmes? What sorts of things has he learnt from television?
- When he was small did parents or other adults read or tell stories to him? How often: never/not very often (less than once a week)/about once a week/a couple of times a week/every day?

- Does an adult still tell/read stories now?
- Does he like to look at books? Any favourites?
- Does he bring books back from school? Do you listen to him reading? Does he want you to?
- Does he belong to the school library?
- Do you buy him books? Does he enjoy choosing them?
- Does X do any of the following at home: play with toys/writing/ drawing/reading/looking at books? If so, how frequently: often/ sometimes/never?

Appendix 3: Parental interview from young fluent readers study

From Clark (1976) (discussed in Chapter 11)

> This schedule, which has been used by a number of my students (modified as appropriate), may help you to plan interviews with parents about their children's reading development, whether advanced or delayed. You may wish to follow initial exploratory open-ended questions with more precise questions at a later stage in the interview, where you offer the parent alternative answers from which to choose. This was planned in the 1960s, therefore there will, I am sure, be additional questions you would want to insert in the light of more recent research findings on early reading development and the increasingly technological environment that even young preschool children experience, with television, videos, computers and even mobile phone texting. One of the reviewers of my book, who had a child who read before starting school, decided to use this interview schedule in relation to his own child and found the responses very interesting.
>   The list of questions below will indicate the range of topics covered.

The precise wording of the questions varied as appropriate. The questions were open-ended and the subsequent classification of answers, planned on the basis of 'pilot' interviews, is shown below. More than one answer could be ticked, and often the exact words used by the parent were included in quotes. Note: for comparative purposes, questions were included about birth, early life and aspects of development which are normally explored in history taking of children with reading difficulties (see Chapter 11).

Although 'he' is used throughout this outline, the same questions were asked concerning boys and girls, with the child's name used.

- How long has be been reading in the way he does now? What was his age at that time?
- What does he like to read at the moment: fiction/non-fiction/adult books/comics/press/everything/other (including puzzle books, poetry)?

- Where does he get his books: school library/public library/bought/ 'inherited'/other?
- Does he belong to a library (other than the school library): YES/NO. If YES, when did he first join?
- How often does he go to the library: weekly/fortnightly/monthly/ occasionally?
- Does he choose his own books or get help: chooses his own/gets help/ both?
- Does anyone read to him now? YES/NO
  If YES, the same or different books?
- Who reads to him: mother/father/sibling/other/all?
- What does he do if he comes to a word he does not know: asks/sounds out/guesses/other?
- Do you often suggest books he would enjoy, or does he enjoy choosing his own? (borrowing and buying)
- How old was he when he started to try to read: 1–2 years/2–3/3–4/4–5?
- At what age did he show an interest in written words and numbers?
- How did he first start to read: by interest prompted by mother in flash cards or alphabet and sounds or word or alphabet games/by interest in observing a sibling or friend learning/by interest in mother or sibling reading aloud/no apparent interest as above but started on blackboard and letter sets or books or press, comics or signs or kitchen packages?
- What were some of the things that interested him in learning to read: to gain information/to emulate siblings/to read posters, packets, etc./ watching television/nothing specific?
- What kind of materials did he use: books/signs/papers?
- Did you ever buy books you thought would help: YES/NO?
  If YES, what kind: picture books/story books/primers/reading scheme/ other?
- When was he first helped?
- What form did the help take?
- Who helped mostly: mother/father/sibling/other?
- How often did they help: daily/weekly/at odd times/when requested?
- Was the help regular or irregular: more systematic/more casual/part of everyday life?
- What kinds of help: told words he asked/comprehension checked/pictures discussed?
- Could he write or print when he first started school: YES/NO?
  If YES, was it printing or writing?
- At what age did he first show an interest in printing and writing?
- At what age did he first write or print?
- How did he start: copying letters or words/writing name/taught at school/ other?

- What kind of materials were used: paper and pencil/backboard and chalks/ plastic letters?
- What kind of help was given: shown how, and hand held/errors corrected/encouragement only/other?
- Did he use capitals or lower case letters?
- What kind of activities did he seem to do well preschool: pencil and paper games and painting/reading/manipulative games/sport and active games/ imaginative?
- With whom did he play mainly: children his own age/younger children/ older children/siblings/no one/other?
- When playing with other children, what did they do: pencil and paper games and painting/reading/manipulative games/sport and active games/ imaginative?
- Was he a leader or a follower?
- Did he prefer to spend his time with adults or children?
- Did he go to nursery school or playgroup?
- Have you read any books about teaching children to read: YES/NO?
- Do you feel his interest in reading was initiated by himself or that you encouraged him to make a start: by child/by parent?
- How did the school react to the child's reading: told/not noticed and had to be told/pleased/indifferent/said it gave scope/said it did not?
- How interested is he in school: extremely/adequately/sometimes/not?
- Have any of your other children read before starting school: YES/NO?
- Are any of the younger children showing any signs of early reading: YES/ NO?
- Did you or your husband read before starting school: YES/NO?
- Do you feel you and your husband read more than average, average, or less?
- What kinds of books do you like to read?
- How old were you when this child was born?
- How old were you when leaving school?
- How old was your husband when leaving school?
- Did either you or your husband pass any public examinations: O level/ A level or Highers/trade/profession? (for mother and father)
- What is your husband's work?
- What was your work when you left school?
- Did you work after marriage?
- Have you worked since you had children: YES/NO?
- If YES: full-time/part-time/occasionally?
- Do you work now: YES/NO?
  If YES: full-time/part-time/occasionally?
  If NO, do you plan to?
- Thinking of your family as a whole, do you feel that any of your children have a closer relationship to you, your husband or any other adult?

- Did this young fluent reader watch television before starting school? If so, how often: seldom/very often/regularly/selectively/non-selectively?
- Are you aware of anything he has learnt from television?

In addition to answering questions on the range of topics indicated above, the parent was asked questions on the following topics (often asked of children with difficulties):

- Early functioning: walking, talking, age on sitting, smiling, use of hands, hearing, vision.
- Laterality of child and parents.
- Family learning and family health.
- Emotional and social behaviour: sleep pattern, crying, nail biting, aggression, temper, fears, bedwetting, wandering, separation from mother and duration.

Index

An indispensable and timely sourcebook for anyone involved in the early years field.' *Ann Lewis, Professor of Special Education and Educational Psychology, University of Birmingham, UK*

t is easy to be blinkered by the pace of change and flood of documents on early education and care, and overlook the insights to be gained from past research.

Using the author's unique approach, this second edition of *Understanding Research in Early Education* examines and discusses both recent and historical research in understandable yet rigorous language, and a wide variety of large- and small-scale research reports and projects are evaluated. Drawing on her own studies, as well as many others, Margaret Clark illustrates how to avoid common pitfalls, ask the right questions to help inform students' own research projects and, critically, apply findings in the classroom or nursery to improve practice.

Without requiring any prior expertise in research and research methodologies, this book will prove invaluable and fascinating reading for undergraduate and postgraduate students taking courses in early years education, and practitioners undertaking continuing professional development.

Margaret M. Clark has an international reputation for research in early education and literacy. She is Emeritus Professor of Education, University of Birmingham and Visiting Professor at Newman College of Higher Education, Birmingham.

EDUCATION/EDUCATION RESEARCH

Routledge
Taylor & Francis Group

www.routledge.com/education   Printed in Great Britain

ISBN 0-415-36113-3

9 780415 361132

O9-BNG-903